BECOMING a Level FIVE Multiplying Church Field Guide

Todd Wilson // Dave Ferguson
Founders of Exponential

With Alan Hirsch

Foreword by
Ed Stetzer

Edited by Lindy Lowry
Foreword by Ed Stetzer
Cover design by Josh Shank and Karen Pheasant
Layout by Eric Reiss and Story.GS

Special Thanks

We want to thank Exponential for their role in making this resource available for free in digital form. They are fantastic partners in ministry. Please check out their website at exponential.org and consider sending them an email of thanks!

Lindy Lowry, Josh Shank, Karen Pheasant and Eric Reiss (story.gs), you were instrumental in helping create this new resource by handling the editing, graphic designs, formatting, and other details of producing and distributing a book. You are the best at what you do.

A diverse team of strategic, futuristic practioners who care deeply about the church and church multiplication have invested time to help develop the content in this book. Thanks to Daniel Im (LifeWay Christian Resources), Jeff Christopherson (NAMB Send Network), Chris Lagerlof (Mission Orange County), Mac Lake (NAMB), Mike McDaniel (The Summit Network), Jeff Shipman (Christ Together), Justin Moxley (Stadia), Winfield Bevins (Asbury Seminary), Bill Easum (21st Century Strategies), and Wade Burnett (MultiSite Solutions).

The creative team at Exponential, including Don Smith, Pat Masek, and Lucas Cortazio, does a masterful job at bringing the annual Exponential theme to life via the main stage programming at the Exponential conferences (the largest annual gatherings of church planting leaders in the world - exponential.org/events).

The team at Exponential: Terri Saliba, Bill Couchenour, Brooks Hamon, and Anna Wilson. Wow! You are the greatest team in America. Your dedication, sacrifice and servant hearts to help church planters make you the heroes to the heroes you serve!

Finally, we would like to thank our wives, Todd's wife Anna and Dave's wife Sue, for their consistent encouragement and support.

Exponential's 2016 Fall Events

EXPONENTIAL WEST 2016

October 3-6 | Los Angeles, CA

Join thousands of leaders for our national west coast event.

- *2000+ Church Planting Leaders*
- *75 Speakers*
- *9 Tracks*
- *7 Pre-conferences*
- *70 Workshops*

NEW! EXPONENTIAL REGIONALS

September 12-13 | Washington D.C.
November 15-16 | Chicago, IL

Experience Exponential 2016 Main Stage Live—including worship and more than 10 speakers in five sessions. Hear from Dave Gibbons, Dave Ferguson, Michael Frost, Efrem Smith, Mark Batterson + more.

Regional highlights include:

- *Interactive breakout sessions with planters on your same journey or in your network.*
- *Less money and time away (1.5 days vs. 4 days) than Exponential East and West.*
- *Easy to bring your whole team for a time of encouragement and learning together.*
- *Face-to-face connecting opportunities with speakers and other church planters.*

BECOMING 5IVE

Learn what it takes to become a Level 5 Multiplying Church.

Register for Exponential's fall events at:
exponential.org/events

Table of Contents

#MultiplicationMatters

Foreword

It's a strange thing seeing something of little importance become a major focus, yet that's exactly my experience with church planting.

I still remember the gatherings of church planters that took place when I first began in the late 80s. Church planting recently had emerged from obscurity, but just barely. National conferences would draw a few hundred people, who often could not get ministry or church jobs elsewhere.

When I fast-forward a few decades and a few church plants later, I see church planting at the forefront of the thinking of missiologists and pastors, both nationally and globally. The rapid increase in church planting is evident across a wide variety of denominations and networks. Simply put, we see a greater number of people engaged in church planting. Furthermore, according to the latest research, the effectiveness of church planting has increased.

Metric after metric is trending in the right direction.

Those national conferences on church planting that used to struggle to fill out a hotel conference room, now pack large arenas in a way that seemed inconceivable only a few years earlier. Actually, the authors of this book co-founded Exponential, the mother of all such conferences.

But this growth is raising other questions and causing us to confront a heartbreaking reality— church planting in North America has accelerated, but has not broken out in a movement.

It's moved from level 1, but it's nowhere near level 5.

Church Planting Movements

Internationally, we've heard much talk about Church Planting Movements, a concept popularized by David Garrison in his 2004 book and now widely embraced by Christian missiologists. The idea that there would be rapid indigenous church reproduction is not merely an academic theory, but an actual practice occurring in locations and cultures around the world. We have studies on the various ethno-linguistic groups who have experienced this type of exponential church growth.

But this gives rise to our concern. Despite our tracking and analyzing these now established Church Planting Movements, we have yet to see one in the West. Herein lies the frustration. How is it that we can see God move in a certain way around the world, but not move in the same way here?

Part of this can be explained sociologically. In an industrialized society, like our own, labor segmentation causes people to assume specialization. Whether we like it or not, people have a hard time believing a mechanic can also be the pastor. In other cultures, this does not present a problem. But in our own, cultural expectations all but prevent exponential growth.

This does not mean, however, that a movement of sorts could not happen here. But in our context, our church planting efforts should target a different goal.

Church Multiplication Movement

If a Church Planting Movement remains out of our reach in the West, what should our aim be?

In *Viral Churches*, Warren Bird and I proposed a Church *Multiplication* Movement. It does not have the exponential growth characteristic of Church Planting Movements, but it has a 50 percent growth in the number of churches in a given year with 50 percent conversion growth that continues to the third generation.

We proposed this because we have seen it within our lifetimes within certain groups, Calvary Chapel and the Vineyard movements for example. However, it has not broken out into wider culture. Those movements need processes and steps to reach further and become what we desire—a catalyst for a fully realized Church Multiplication Movement in the West.

A multiplication movement does not simply appear fully formed without any work. God will bring the harvest, but He calls for the workers to go out into the fields. Churches, networks, and denominations can do the work to prepare for a harvest from a Church Multiplication Movement.

Though certainly not an exhaustive list, I believe there are five basics that would help make multiplication movements a higher priority and much more likely within many denominations.

First, you need leaders who share the vision to build momentum. Pastors, denominational and network leaders cannot make a movement, but they can shape the culture of a movement by empowering and celebrating the right leaders. Having persuasive, passionate leaders out at the forefront calling others to join them is a great place to start.

Second, success stories need to be found and trumpeted. Stories grant the information an emotional connection, which is why the gospel is the greatest story ever told. To help the movement pick up steam, find and tell stories of the impact church plants have had on communities and individuals.

Third, remember that what you celebrate, you become. If you want to encourage church planting, inspire the people of your congregation, take opportunities to celebrate church planters and those who are multiplying the work of Kingdom building.

Fourth, nothing can splash cold water on a tiny spark of a movement quite like someone dismissing or undermining the church planting work. There needs to be buy-in across the people of God if a Church Multiplication Movement is to succeed.

Fifth, we need to trust and follow the Spirit as He, in accordance to His word, births a disciple making movement that becomes an exponential movement toward multiplication.

But even with those five steps, we need some concept of progress or evaluation. How can a church know it's on the right track?

That's where this book comes in. The idea of progressive levels of involvement and success presented in the following pages are key to understanding the journey to a movement. Here in *Becoming a Level Five Multiplying Church Field Guide*, we find this concept laid forth in an easy to understand manner.

The book is intended to provide a rubric and language to help your church become more effective at multiplication—ultimately moving us toward movement. Furthermore, the idea of multiplication levels gives us steps and informs and challenges us to greater movemental focus, helpful to create a process with a new scorecard.

Churches can determine on what level they currently reside and take steps to advance until they reach the fifth and final level. When churches and leaders grasp the next step to take, it enables movements to not only become a goal, but an attainable goal and, at some point, a realized goal.

I'm thankful for the contribution Todd Wilson and Dave Ferguson have made to that end with this book.

~Ed Stetzer

Multiplication Quiz

We realize most books don't open with a quiz. But we promise this one is painless and takes less than two minutes of your time to complete. And we believe identifying or assessing what you really think or believe about multiplication is invaluable for taking in and using this book.

For this Multiplication Quiz, read through the following statements and using the ratings scale below, identify how strongly you agree with each statement by selecting 1 through 5. In the margin next to each question, note your rating. For example, if you strongly agree with question 1, jot down a "5":

Multiplication Quiz

Use these ratings:

1 strongly disagree
2 disagree
3 neutral
4 agree
5 strongly agree

Statement Number	My Score (1 - 5)
S1	Multiplication is the central New Testament pattern, and yet in the U.S. we have a hard time advancing beyond an addition mentality.
S2	Church multiplication must be lauded as a worthy and achievable goal by those not in the middle of it. We must lift up church planting multipliers as heroes of church leadership in our day.

S3	The more that churches in the U.S. grow, the more likely they grow by addition rather than multiplication.
S4	A massive multiplication movement of new church planting would likely have a greater impact than doubling the number of megachurches.
S5	When we commit to plant, and do, the church we plant will outlast us. No other strategy guarantees that.
S6	Addition doesn't always lead to reproduction, but reproduction always leads to addition.
S7	Reproduction does not always lead to multiplication, but multiplication always leads to reproduction.
S8	Addition does not always yield multiplication, but multiplication always yields addition.
S9	Focus on reproducing for multiplication, and you will add. Focus on adding to grow, and you might add.
S10	Our church multiplication in the U.S. is hindered because we have a scorecard for addition!

* Several of the statements above are derived from quotes by Ed Stetzer, Warren Bird and Rick Warren in *Viral Churches: Helping Church Planters Become Movement Makers* by Ed Stetzer and Warren Bird (Jossey-Bass).

Now, add up your total score on these 10 questions. The minimum total score is 10 points (10 x 1) with a maximum score of 50 possible points (10 x 5). Now divide your total score by 10 to get your aspirational or final average score (your final score will be between 1 and 5).

Between Aspiration and Practice

When we took this quiz, our point totals were 50. We "strongly agreed" with every statement about church multiplication put forth in these questions. So our aspirational average score is 5 (50 divided by 10)! We're guessing yours is also a 4+. We use the word "aspirational" here because we think you'll agree that our aspiration is to be part of movements—characterized by a final score of 5 on this quiz. We yearn to be part of movements that multiply the way Jesus intended.

To be a movement is part of the deepest instincts of the church. This is because the church's mission always drives us to transfer the Message that we hold in ways that reach our immediate cultures and beyond that, to the ends of the earth. The only way the church can do this is through the *movemental* form. Thankfully, it is the form of the church that we find in our primary documents...the New Testament.

Alan's Insight

So why do so few of us find ourselves part of Level 5 multiplying churches? Our problem is not aspirational. Instead, it's rooted in the things that cause a gap between our aspirations and our practices. We inevitably encounter tensions that hold us back from multiplication.

Now, read the 10 questions again. This time, think about the specific realities and factors in the life of a church and its leaders—things that cause a gap between our aspirations and our practices.

In the 2014 Exponential book *Spark: Igniting a Culture of Multiplication*, I (Todd) highlighted how the prevailing addition-growth cultures shape and define our scorecards for success. The priorities and behaviors of an addition-focused scorecard help us grow and break the next attendance barrier. Yet they eventually

17

become the things holding us back from experiencing the multiplication we were designed for.

Now, take a second short quiz. This time, rate the questions based on the reality of how the average church in America answers and lives out these statements:

Behaviors of Multiplication Quiz

Use these ratings:

1 strongly disagree
2 disagree
3 neutral
4 agree
5 strongly agree

Statement Number	My Score (1 - 5)

S1   The average church has a church planting intern/resident in training who will launch a new church within the next 12 months.

S2   The average church leader is more focused on multiplying new churches than they are on growing their own church larger and conquering the next attendance barrier.

S3   The average church leader tithes (at least 10 percent) the first fruits of their budget to church planting.

S4   The average church leader plants their first autonomous church before assuming land and building debt.

S5   The average church leader plants their first autonomous church before launching their own first campus or multi-site.

S6   The average church has a specific plan for doubling their church planting activity.

S7   The average church leader releases/sends out their first church planter before accumulating their first three staff members (and then continues to release at least one planter per year for every three staff members).

S8   The average church leader visibly and regularly calls their members to go and be part of a church planting team.

S9   The average church leader visibly and regularly calls their members to give sacrificially above and beyond their tithe to the local church to support church plants.

S10   The average church is actively affiliated with and participating in a church planting network (or denominational initiative) pursuing multiplication.

Just as you did on the first quiz, add up your total score on these 10 questions. Again, there are a minimum of 10 points (10 x 1) and a maximum of 50 possible points (10 x 5). Now divide your total by 10 to get your score (final score will be between 1 and 5).

If you're like us, you "strongly disagreed" with most of these statements, and your final score is 1 (10 divided by 10)!

The first quiz focused on what we'd like to see in the future, so we scored high (4+). The second quiz focusing on behaviors offers a rearview mirror look at the practices of most churches, so we scored low.

Notice how the practices reflected in the 10 questions of the second quiz are the types of behaviors needed to fulfill the aspirations in the first quiz. Unfortunately, we have a large gap between behaviors and aspirations! So what can we do about it?

The Gap

Alan's Insight

Our first step in organizational learning is to acknowledge that there is a problem. This requires that we acknowledge the current situation honestly. And if need be…to be willing to "repent" by letting go of obsolete practices and ideas so that we might more faithfully create new practices more appropriate to the challenges of the 21st century.

Courageous leaders discover and acknowledge the gap between aspiration and practice AND act to do something about it.

Our mission and commitment at Exponential is to champion multiplication and equip church multipliers. This book is a manifesto of sorts that we believe will help us define a practical vocabulary and framework that courageous leaders like you can rally behind and grab onto as you seek to close the gap between your aspirations for multiplication and the strong tensions that constrain you to addition-growth thinking.

Be courageous! As you read through this book, continue to ask yourself: *What would it take to face and overcome the tensions that are keeping me from living out a better scorecard rooted in multiplication?*

Close the gap!

Introduction
Continuing the Multiplication
Conversation

Becoming a Level Five Multiplying Church continues a conversation started in the 2014 Exponential book *Spark: Igniting a Culture of Multiplication.* Think of it as a sequel of sorts that drills down into more detail focusing on how we can each play our part in moving the needle on church multiplication.

By focusing on the need to be a multiplying church, we are forced to think differently than what we have become all too accustomed to…addition thinking. Think of this as a big hairy goal.

Alan's Insight

As we pressed into our Exponential 2015 theme of igniting a culture of multiplication, our team set out to identify 10 radically multiplying U.S. churches—just 10 that we could highlight and learn from. With more than 350,000 churches in the United States, that 10 represents just .003 percent of churches. We spent months searching for them, but we couldn't find 10.

We couldn't find even three.

Something's not right. This isn't how it's meant to be. The gap between aspiration and practices highlighted in the Multiplication Quiz in the previous section certainly burdens God's heart. Closing this gap is worth giving our lives to and committing our resources. What will it take to move the needle from less than 0.05 percent to greater than 10 percent (and beyond)?

At Exponential, we dream about closing this gap and hitting a tipping point where multiplication becomes mainstream and evolves into the new normal that leaders aspire to and pursue.

To close the gap between our aspirations and our current paradigm, we need to look hard at our motives, our measures, and our methods. Are these elements rooted in a core value of multiplication? How do we learn to put to death our human passion for addition-growth, opting instead for a more healthy Kingdom growth focused on multiplication?

Alan's Insight Beyond looking at our motives, metrics and methods, we need to learn how to actually change the church paradigm. We should also take a long, hard look at the rationale supporting our old ways of thinking. Bottom line: We need to be willing to recalibrate. (Check out Dave and Alan's book *On The Verge* for ways in which leaders can change the paradigm.)

While you'll see some of the same thoughts and insights in this new book, we encourage you to download and read *Spark: Igniting a Culture of Multiplication* to get a full context for this new book. *Spark* is available for FREE download here (exponential.org).

Moving the Needle on Multiplication

What will it take to move the needle on multiplication and close the gap between our aspirations and our practices? We believe at least five actions are required:

#1 - *Embrace a core value and culture of multiplication.*
Our values are the vital factors that shape what we do and how we do it. We must develop a heart and passion for multiplication. Not simply a value on paper, but instead a deeply engrained priority that we live out every day. A compass that shapes our thinking and guides our decision-making.

What culture are you creating in your church? Be honest. Not the seemingly elusive culture you *want* to develop, but rather the *real* culture you're creating by your thinking, actions, and the models you pursue. Are you developing a subtraction, survival, and scarcity culture: "We will [fill in blank] *after* we grow or can afford it." Or maybe an addition-growth culture characterized by an insatiable drive for conquering the next hill and breaking the next growth barrier: "Where is the next one?" Or are you bucking the norm and creating a multiplication-growth culture? A culture best characterized by release versus consumption, and movement versus accumulation?

Exponential's 2015 theme, "Spark," highlighted three key elements of a healthy, aligned culture:

Our Culture = Our Core Values + Our Narratives + Our Behaviors
Let's look at each one.

It has rightly been said that "culture eats strategy for breakfast." Because of this, we had better pay attention to it. Having said that, changing culture takes real vision, commitment, patience, and process. But change at this level will change everything.

Alan's Insight

Core values ... the things so important to us that they shape how we think and how we do all that we do. Our core values reflect our heart, what we really care about deep down. They overflow to shape the words of our mouth (our narrative) and the actions of our hands (our behaviors).

Narratives... the language we use, the stories we tell, and how frequently we talk about and celebrate the things most important to us. Our narratives inspire others to embrace our values and engage on common mission with us.

Behaviors ... the things we actually do, including how and where we invest the time, talent, and financial resources entrusted to our care.

Spark introduced these three core elements of culture and now with *Becoming a Level Five Multiplying Church*, we want to press more deeply into how we live them out.

#2 - *Embrace a new scorecard and paradigm for measuring "healthy growth."*

This practice moves us beyond the ornery and unhealthy parts of our scorecard that are entrenched in addition and accumulation paradigms. *Spark* introduced a framework for "healthy growth," and now *Becoming a Level Five Multiplying Church* expands on that framework (see chapter 2: Rethinking Healthy Growth). Our understanding of healthy growth is a game changer in understanding how addition-growth can derail and inhibit multiplication-growth. Dave's free eBook, *Keeping Score: How to Know If Your Church Is Winning*, available through Exponential (exponential.org/resource-ebooks/), offers a strong supplemental resource.

#3 - *Embrace the specific behaviors and decisions characteristic of multiplying churches.*

We need a framework or standard we can turn to that describes the profile and characteristics of the behaviors of multiplying churches. The simple 10-question "Behaviors of Multiplication" quiz at the beginning of this book is an example of defining just a few characteristics and behaviors of multiplying churches. Think about this: *If just 10 percent of the churches attending an Exponential conference each year committed to the practices reflected in the quiz questions, the trajectory of Christianity in the U.S. would change.*

Unfortunately, most churches aspire to become like the prominent addition-growth churches they hear and read about. Without strong multiplication role models, leaders have no one to coach and mentor them in the values and practices characteristic of multiplying churches.

Alan's Insight

Almost all of the books and authors that define what is "successful" come from deep within the addition mindset...in fact they are its guardians. Herein lies much of our problem...we get what we aim for. You have to think differently to act differently.

In this book, we look at the reality and context of a wide spectrum of U.S. churches, ranging from those in survival/subtraction mode to addition/growth mode and then finally to multiplication. You'll find profiles for five different levels of church multiplication, including descriptions and characteristics of each one. Most leaders can simply read through the profiles and discern their church's level.

We also have created the vocabulary, profiles, and characteristics that form the core of a new assessment tool that can be used by any church to discern their level of multiplication (visit exponential.org/level5 to take the free assessment). This tool was designed to help you assess where you are and then make adjustments into the future to move toward becoming a Level 5 multiplying church. Chapter 3 introduces the five levels of multiplying churches. You'll also want to check out the appendix for the descriptions of each profile.

#4 - Understand and manage the key tensions that can be barriers to multiplication.

All churches face tension. None are immune. As churches progress from Level 1 up to Level 5, they will face a multitude of different tensions. Most are predictable. These tensions are responsible for the bulk of the gap between our aspirations and our behaviors. How we respond to and deal with these tensions defines how we answer those 10 behavioral questions from the second quiz.

Spark introduced more than 15 different tensions that churches seeking to become multiplying churches will face. In this new book, we've grouped these tensions and distilled them down to three key ones all churches will face in moving to Level 5. These tensions include:

- **Tension of Motives**: "*Here* or *There*"
  This tension is rooted in our definition of success. Is our vision limited to accumulating and growing larger *here*, or is it balanced with an equal focus and passion for sending *there*? This tension is rooted in the values embedded in a church's DNA. The definition of success that moves a church from Level 1 or 2 (subtracting or plateaued) to Level 3 (addition) reflects a different value system than the one that moves a church to Level 4 and 5. To move through

26

this tension, we must embrace and become passionate about the value of multiplication. We must balance here *and* there.

This is what our good friend Bob Roberts Jr., refers to as having a *glocal* vision of the church. To think "glocally" requires that we think in terms of the global obligation to the nations but learn to act locally in light of that call. This understanding of mission is at the heart of New Testament understandings of the church and will lead directly to thinking of the church in terms of multiplication and scalability.

Alan's Insight

- ***Tension of Measures***: *"Grow or Send"*
  This tension is rooted in our priority of focus: Where do we focus our time, talent and treasure? Growing *here* or sending *there*? The same staff and finances that can help us grow *here* are the ones needed to send *there*. As our local platform increases, our capacity for even greater sending grows. Unfortunately, most churches adopt a "we will send after we grow and have the resources" approach. We must balance growing *and* sending.

- ***Tension of Methods***: *"Safety or Risk"*
  What will we actually do (and what hard decisions will we make) to become a Level 5 multiplying church? Good intentions will not move us from Level 1 to 5. We only change by *doing* what we say we want to do. Until you are able to not only strongly agree with the questions in the multiplication quizzes—but then put them into practice— you will not become a multiplying church.

Alan's Insight

Because movements must be entrepreneurial and ultimately extend the frontiers of the church, they will always find a way to develop and maintain a risk-taking culture. Risk and adventure are as much a part of the biblical definition of faith as they are characteristics of a Level 5 movement. Risks need not to be death-defying to be valuable. But without some risk, the church will inevitably flounder and become unfaithful.

Whether or not you realize it, you are creating and cultivating a culture in your church. There is no stopping it. Just as the sun rises and sets each day, your core values and convictions are always there, transforming your thinking into actions that functionally form your church's unique culture. How you face and maneuver through the tensions you experience might be the most significant blessings you have in shaping your church's culture and DNA.

Like the small rudder on a large ship directing the ship's course, the stewardship of the culture/DNA in your church may be the most profound role you play as its leader. Tensions are inseparable from the culture you cultivate. Embrace them as a blessing.

#5 - *Live out your culture with intentionality, focus, urgency and an abundance mindset.*
Your specific culture (subtraction, addition, or multiplication) is formed not by who you want to be in the future, but rather by who you are and what you're doing today. Each of the small, consistent daily decisions you make is a stone in the foundation of the culture you foster. Want a multiplication culture in your church? Figure out how to multiply in your context *now*. Research shows us that when a church waits for an elusive day in the future to start leaning into multiplication, that elusive day never comes.

Just like an orchard is contained in a single apple, so movement-potential is fully contained in the initiating organization. The same is true for making right decisions, made up of a long series of right decisions in the right direction. Don't worry about starting small. Decisions with the right DNA eventually produce the right tree.

Alan's Insight

As we've said before, it takes courageous leadership to overcome the prevailing addition-growth cultures that have become our measure of success. Courageous leaders will acknowledge and address head-on each of the above tensions. A leader with a multiplication mindset has the opportunity to define and shape the future landscape of Christianity in the West.

Objectives

Our objectives in writing this book are narrowly focused. We want to champion multiplication and equip future church multipliers to move beyond our prevailing addition-growth scorecards. Specifically, *Becoming a Level Five Multiplying Church* seeks to:

- continue the multiplication conversation that *Spark* began during the Exponential 2015 theme cycle into Exponential 2016;

- introduce a new framework and vocabulary for multiplying churches, including a framework for balancing addition and multiplication for healthy growth; and a second framework for discerning five different levels of multiplication;

Language is a vital part of culture…change the language and the culture will change as people grapple to come to grips with what it means within the group. Consistently use the words "multiplication" and "movement" and eventually it will all make sense to everyone in the organization.

Alan's Insight

- introduce a new assessment tool for helping leaders discern which of the five levels of multiplication (Levels 1 - 5) their church is currently living out;

- stress the vital importance of biblical disciple making as our primary measure of success, and as the fuel for multiplication. Highlight that the fruit of biblical disciple making must produce disciples who GO;

- highlight three core tensions that all leaders will face in their journey toward becoming a Level 5 multiplying church.

As you think toward the future of what it means for you and your church to embrace multiplication and build a new scoreboard, my prayer is that you grasp what it looks like to become a multiplying church that measures success by making biblical disciples who GO, as well as take action to be the courageous leader of one.

Let's get started!

Chapter 1
Rethinking Our Operating System

Unless you've lived under a rock for the last 15 years, you probably have a smart phone (or know someone who does). Within seconds you can connect with anyone in your address book on your smart phone, and you can access just about any information you need via the Internet. You can even ask your phone questions and get remarkably reliable answers.

Reflect on how and why your phone consistently produces those results. At its core, three elements combine to give us consistently good experiences with smart phones:

Hardware + Software + Operating System = Consistent Results

The hardware is the tangible thing we hold in our hands. We see it, hold it, and interact with it. It comes in all shapes, sizes, and colors but at its core are a screen, buttons, memory, processor and other electrical components. Hardware is a platform or container for software to do its heavy lifting.

The software resides inside and is programmed to interact with humans and the hardware. Software is designed and manipulated to produce desired outcomes.

The operating system provides a framework for the hardware and the software to interact and play together nicely. It's the orchestra conductor communicating the rules and guidelines for how the hardware and software interact to consistently produce the results we're looking for. The operating system provides a context for a wide variety of different software applications to work within the hardware.

This "operating system" metaphor is an important one that helps us understand how movements are formed. Everything usable is built on the OS platform. Think about the *Uber* platform - a multibillion-dollar taxi company that doesn't own a single taxi! An exercise: Sketch out a picture of how you think Uber *really* works.

Alan's Insight

Over the past 20 years we've watched the technological advancement from pager, to analog handheld device, to several generations of data-capable smart phones. Each advancement simply aligns hardware, software and an operating system in new ways to produce a desired result.

Throughout our everyday lives, we encounter numerous other examples where consistent outcomes—from ordering coffee at Starbucks to waiting for the synchronous change of green, yellow and red lights at an intersection—is the product of hardware, software and an operating system interacting in harmony together.

In this way, most things in life are perfectly designed to deliver the consistent results we see. If we don't like the results we're getting in some area of life, we should start by looking carefully at the alignment of the elements that make up our operating systems.

Our deep burden in writing this book is the lack of healthy church multiplication happening in the U.S. church. Approximately 80 percent of U.S. churches are either plateaued or declining. Flip it around, and this stat tells us that only 20 percent are growing. Now think about this. Of those growing churches, less than 4 percent are reproducing, and well under 0.5 percent (essentially 0 percent) are multiplying as a consistent and regular product of their operating systems.

The prevailing operating systems that give us church growth are falling short of giving us church multiplication. Through survival of the fittest, the current system sets its sights on accumulation and addition-growth. We are adding, but are we adding in a way that produces the transformation needed for multiplication?

Alan's Insight

An apple tree does not produce oranges. The current operating systems of the church are not designed to produce multiplication. In fact, they are perfectly designed to produce what they are currently producing …subtraction or addition. The key to change is therefore updating the operating system so that it can produce movement. It is sobering to note that the early church naturally experienced high impact apostolic movement.

Several decades ago the operating system for planting churches changed. Peter Drucker, the father of modern management, had an indirect impact on the emerging church growth movement. At the core of Drucker's work in the marketplace are three simple yet profound questions: Who is our customer? What do they value? How do we deliver that value?

The best companies have aligned their strategies to an operating system that delivers alignment on these three core questions. This customer service posture has also helped fuel the church growth movement. By focusing on who the lost people in our communities are, and understanding what they value, we can design church to attract and serve these people.

The strength of the megachurch (where we see most of the numerical growth in U.S. churches) is rooted in operating systems that align and scale the institution and resources of the local church (the hardware) with addition-oriented activities and strategies (the software) to target and meet the perceived needs of the customer. The mega-church's strength is its attracting capacity, as resourced through staff, buildings, programs, excellent Sunday services and preaching, marketing and outreach events.

This operating system values a scalable, transactional approach to adding whereby we "score" when we attract the customer, and they choose to stick around. Unfortunately, this transactional customer focused system also set us up to spend increasing amounts of time and energy seeking to appease our customers and keep them sticking around.

This is a fatal flaw in the system - it is not built to produce disciples but rather to attract and retain religious consumers (what you win them with, you win them to). Conversely, every movement that changed the world has a primary emphasis on discipleship and disciple making. If you are not producing disciples, **Alan's Insight** then the problem is in the design of the system. A correction at this point will make all the difference.

Pause and reflect on the potential unintended consequences. We are called to make biblical disciples who GO as an expression of their increasing maturity. Too often we are building churches that spend most of their time attracting, appeasing, and seeking to keep cultural Christians sticking around. Yes, this is a harsh assessment, but part of courageous leadership is embracing the truths of our present realities that produce essentially 0 percent of U.S. churches multiplying.

Customer-focused operating systems are also great when you're selling televisions or cars and need to close the deal with a transaction. But how would things be different if companies like Ford and Apple measured success not by a transaction but instead by the transformation of those they reach?

What if the fuel to healthy growth came through transformation rather than transaction? What if the lack of multiplication we see in the U.S. church is actually a reflection of the quality of our disciple making? What if we have to make biblical disciples who have a natural impulse to GO as they more fully mature? What if our zeal for accumulation is unintentionally making cultural Christians who continually need to be fed rather than biblical disciples who actually fuel multiplication and movements?

We believe that the strengths of this current operating system—attracting and connecting with people far from God—are essential and to be celebrated. But we're deeply convicted that the prevailing operating system that new church planters so passionately embrace also has shortcomings in producing the transformation needed to both fuel and sustain multiplication movements.

In the end, we get what we initially wanted. "If you want to see churches planted, then you must set out to plant churches... If you want to see reproducing churches planted, then you must set out to plant reproducing churches" (David Garrison). Again the issue takes us to the design. Pay attention to the system!

Alan's Insight

The current system is perfectly aligned to give us accumulation and addition-growth. What if, instead, we could have addition-growth that actually fuels multiplication? What if, instead of accumulating larger stockpiles, we became catalysts for deploying and sending biblical disciples?

We must put biblical disciple making squarely at the core of our measure of success. Holistically, its what we are commanded to DO while simultaneously being the fuel that powers multiplication.

We stand at a crossroads in history with the opportunity to pilot a better future. But to make this revolutionary change, we need to rethink our current operating systems and becoming courageous leaders willing to discover and embrace new ones.

This book is positioned as a "field guide" to help leaders compare and contrast the differences between subtraction, addition and multiplication cultures. A field guide is typically used "in the field" (or by practitioners) to understand the differences between different things. For example, a field guide can help us see and discern the subtle distinctions between different birds—minor distinctions but ones that make all the difference to an avid birdwatcher or ornithologist.

Field guides are often descriptive and illustrative. They go deeper than simple narratives but fall short of providing detailed instructions, stories and roadmaps. These reference guides focus on the foundational, factual, technical differences between things for characterization purposes rather than stories for inspiration.

In *Becoming a Level Five Multiplying Church Field Guide*, we intentionally focus on descriptions and language rather than stories. You may find yourself saying, "This feels technical ... give me more stories and examples of the different levels of multiplication!" Be patient. This book is a manifesto of sorts and intended to provide a simple framework and a vocabulary from which a new and expanding library of multiplication resources emerge. These new resources will highlight the stories and examples you're longing for.

Alan's Insight

Futurist Alvin Toffler is known for his observation: "You've got to think about big things while you're doing small things, so that all the small things go in the right direction." Movement thinking provides an organization with a larger context, model and a larger vision - a strategic framework for organizing facts and discerning patterns.

Finally, you may be a cynic, easily distracted by your skepticism for the credibility of research data. We want to encourage you not to let specific numbers keep you from seeing the underlying truths that the numbers point to. The bottom line is that our current, prevailing operating systems are not producing reproduction and multiplication as a normal outcome. You already intuitively know that, so don't let specific research numbers distract you from the more important truths and the need for change.

For example:

- We cite Ed Stetzer and Warren Bird's statistic from their book *Viral Churches* (Jossey Bass) that 80 percent of U.S. churches are plateaued or declining.
- From this 80 percent, we can then conclude that 20 percent of U.S. churches are growing.
- We cite a March 24, 2011 NAMB report that 4 percent of Southern Baptist churches ever reproduce. We assume the 4 percent are part of the 20 percent of churches that are growing.
- For months, the Exponential team surveyed churches and looked hard to find just 10 rapidly multiplying churches. We could not find three. In *Viral Churches*, Stetzer and Bird were unable to find many. We assume based on this experience that the number of churches multiplying as part of their DNA is much less than 0.5 percent of all U.S. churches.
- From the above, we can deduce that approximately 16 percent of churches are growing but are not reproducing or multiplying.

In summary, 80 percent are plateaued or declining; 16 percent are adding but not reproducing or multiplying; 4 percent are reproducing but are not multiplying; and essentially 0 percent are multiplying.

The bottom line ... we need to rethink the operating system that's producing growth but is not producing multiplication. Let's start by taking a fresh look at our personal definitions of healthy growth.

Chapter 2
Rethinking Healthy Growth

*"Be fruitful and increase in number;
multiply on the earth and increase upon it." ~ God*

In Exponential's 2014 book, *Spark: Igniting a Culture of Multiplication*, we introduced several core concepts, including the idea that movements occur at the intersection between addition and multiplication. Movements multiply through addition, with life-on-life and one-on-one relationships offering the best context for adding disciples.

The principles for this come from Jesus and His Commission to make disciples (Matt. 28:19). We must have a local or "micro" strategy that is both reproducible *and* works at the individual disciple level. The reality is that all multiplication has addition at its core: reaching the "next one."

The gospels show us how Jesus handed down a model of personal discipleship and evangelism—a model that we would say is solid addition-growth. In the local church, we need a strategy that creates environments where each and every follower of Jesus can participate in addition-growth with a focus on their personal sphere of influence.

At the same time, we must simultaneously and intentionally embrace a strategy that looks beyond our local context and seeks to extend and multiply churches. This strategy recognizes that the most powerful way to multiply is to equip and send leaders who create new churches, which become platforms for addition at the individual believer level.

Another way of paraphrasing this strategy is: "You must have a micro or local strategy close to home for *adding* the next one, and simultaneously a macro strategy for *multiplying* your impact beyond your local context." The two must work in synergy with the *adding* fueling the *multiplying*.

Go back to Genesis. Noah repopulated the earth with a micro/ macro strategy. Micro-addition adds new family members (children). When they reach maturity and are capable of reproducing themselves (adults), the macro sets in. Children leave their mother and father and start their own families, reproducing through a model handed down to them over generations. The process continues to repeat itself.

Alan's Insight

Movement thinking sees the potential for the whole in even the smallest part. Discipleship is the very basic building block of the church. Just like an apple seed houses the full potential for an apple tree, the possibility for a church lies in every disciple. How else can we explain the early church? The challenge for multiplication leaders is to first "see" this amazing truth, and then to "act" on that truth.

God designed His church to function in the same way! The micro (or local) does the heavy lifting of adding one member at a time, while the macro (releasing and sending) brings the context for multiplying. It takes a unique culture to fuel multiplication and movements thinking.

But what happens when our micro and macro strategies are both focused on addition? Or if we go back to Noah, what happens when he wants to repopulate the earth by being the father of one huge growing family rather than sending his offspring to start new families? Simple. We stunt multiplication. We create the gap between aspirations and practices that we talked about earlier in the Introduction.

While the thought of Noah repopulating the earth on his own seems ludicrous and obviously unnatural, that is exactly what we try to do in the U.S. church with our micro-addition/macro-addition approach. We build and grow ever-larger churches that rarely reproduce.

If we keep applying the same solution/approach to every problem we face, eventually we create huge problems that can't be fixed without a paradigm shift in thinking.

Alan's Insight

In *Spark* we sought to highlight the realities of our prevailing macro-addition strategies and the associated consequences. Now in this new book, our goal is to build on that earlier work and provide a more complete framework for looking at healthy Kingdom growth.

The expanded framework covered in the remainder of this chapter provides a foundation from which we build the profiles of multiplying churches that we're highlighting in chapter 3.

Multiplying What?

I (Todd) am part of is a strong church planting church. Several years ago, we began dreaming about what it might look like to play a role in tripling the number of church plants in our geographic area within the next five years.

To do that, we first had to establish a baseline. How many churches had been started there in the past five years? We spent months hoping to find and connect with every church plant we could.

Good news and bad news. We found approximately 270 churches planted in the previous five years that were still in existence. The bad news ... we did not want to reproduce and triple what we found with any of these 270 churches.

For those of us championing multiplication, this search represents a grand paradox. It's the "elephant in the room" question for all of us: If God blessed our efforts and we were wildly successful at multiplying churches, would we really want to continue reproducing what we are currently producing?

We reproduce who and what we are, what we know and what we value. We must at least consider the possibility that one reason we are not seeing our multiplication efforts lead to movements in the U.S. is because *what* we're producing is not naturally able to multiply (or something that God might not want multiplied).

Movement leader Neil Cole reminds us that if all Americans suddenly decided they didn't need more people but better people, they would never have babies again. Instead, we'd concentrate on the people who already existed. But without children, the U.S. population would collapse in one or two generations. Reproduction is built into all living systems, including the church.

Alan's Insight

Take some time to reflect on these questions:
• What if our core problem is the quality of disciples we're making?
• What if how we're doing church is producing that poor quality?
• Further, what if our macro-addition scorecards and associated strategies are actually the biggest contributors to us building larger and larger pools of cultural Christians?
• What if the way we're starting churches and the scorecards by which we measure success have set us up to birth new churches that accumulate more cultural Christians—new churches that seldom reproduce and send biblical Christians to *go* and multiply?

Over time, we tend to be perfectly aligned to produce the results we get. If we're unhappy with the quality of disciples we're producing and the resulting type of growth we see, the harsh reality is that we have only ourselves to blame. We must start by looking hard at our personal scorecards for healthy Kingdom growth.

Alan's Insight

What got us "here" will not get us "there" if "there" is multiplication. Leadership must take responsibility for the results currently being achieved. This, in turn, leads us to repentance - the paradigm shift needed to reorient the system. Repentance also brings about the necessary unlearning and new learning required to achieve a desired outcome. Assuming responsibility is therefore actually the first step towards real and lasting change. Refusing to take responsibility means that we hand over the organization to the forces that got us to this point in the first place. Repentance - individual and corporate - is a gift from God.

As you read through the rest of this chapter, take time to pause and reflect on the truths, checkpoints and action points. Allow this chapter to be a self-assessment of sorts to help you reflect on your church's foundation. Is it a foundation aligned to produce biblical disciples and multiplication? If not, what adjustments are needed?

Our Motives and Target

On weekends, you might find me (Todd) in my backyard shooting tin cans with a toy BB gun. The gun has a scope on it that's functionally similar to what you've probably seen in TV shows and movies. The vertical and horizontal cross hairs intersect to form the "bulls-eye."

The simple idea is to look through the scope, center the tin can on the cross hairs, pull the trigger, and hit the target. Score!

This may seem obvious, but we hit whatever we're actually aiming at—the thing that is truly at the intersection of the cross hairs. Not simply what we *think* we are aiming at. The challenge is to ensure the right target is at the center.

Jesus Christ at the Start, End and In Between

This goes without saying, but just in case ... healthy growth (both individually and in churches) starts with Jesus Christ, ends with Jesus Christ, and is all about Jesus Christ. Remove Jesus from the core, and we might as well be talking about scaling organizations like Starbucks, Walmart or Apple. So in the framework discussed on the following pages, the given is that Jesus is always and always should be at the core of our motivation and focus.

Remove Jesus from the church and we could well end up with a movement as evil as ISIS or Al Qaeda! It has happened throughout Christian history. Jesus sets the agenda of the whole Jesus movement and is the constant reference point for everything the church says and does.

Alan's Insight

Our friend and author Alan Hirsch is passionate about movement dynamics. In his book, *Forgotten Ways*, Alan highlights six key elements of biblical movements. The core element? *Jesus is Lord!* Regardless of your background, affiliation, context, model or approach, we can all be united in the truth that the core of healthy Kingdom growth is Jesus!

Making His name more famous and seeing billions of people not just saying a prayer or calling on His name, but also surrendering to and living under His authority and Lordship, is the heartbeat of our conviction and the *target* we must put at the center of our multiplication cross hairs.

Truth #1: Our target matters. What we define as success and what we aim at is what we will hit. If we aim for multiplication

44

movements characterized by growing numbers of biblical disciples fully surrendered to Jesus, but get something else, we must first ask ourselves if we're focused on the right target.

Checkpoint #1: Is it possible that our addition-growth scorecards are hitting the wrong target? Could we think we're focused on making disciples of Jesus and willing to die for Him, but in actuality we're focused on other trophies that produce comfortable spiritual seekers and cultural Christians?

Action point #1: What evidence can you show that says you have the right target and that you're producing biblical disciples as a normal expression of your core purpose as a church? Is there any convicting evidence that you're producing safe havens for spiritual seekers and country clubs for cultural Christians?

An exercise: Briefly define what a disciple is and think about exactly how you go about ensuring that disciples are being made in and through your church. It's all in the definition and process of our system. If you think discipleship is about receiving and imparting knowledge about the Bible and attending corporate worship, then you'll likely have a system perfectly designed to produce those results.

Alan's Insight

Aligning the Cross Hairs

Below, Todd describes his experience after getting his BB gun:

When I first got my BB gun, I couldn't hit the target no matter how hard I tried. I'd steadily line up the cross hairs but every time miss the can. I even tried clamping the gun in place to ensure the target was properly centered and that my hand movements weren't causing the inaccuracy.

I can't be this bad, I thought, as I kept missing over and over again. Eventually, I began to suspect a problem with the calibration or alignment of the scope. Sure enough! Turns out that the cross hairs must be adjusted within the viewfinder using small alignment screws on the scope. One screw moves the vertical line left and right while a second screw moves the horizontal line up and down.

Right target + wrong cross hairs = miss the mark!

The same equation applies to your church. When the cross hairs that shape our strategies and actions are wrong or misaligned, we can put Jesus and making biblical disciples squarely in the middle of our sights and yet still miss the mark!

Alan's Insight

If the whole point of the enterprise is to produce disciples - and it's difficult to find a resulting metric more important that that for the church - then we'll need a major alignment of the systems we're currently producing.

Truth #2: The cross hairs matter. They should be our true guides for hitting the target. If our aligning values and core elements for healthy growth are off center, no amount of effort will produce the results we want. Our aspirations will deviate from our behaviors.

Checkpoint #2: Is it possible that our addition growth-focused cross hairs contribute to us missing the target of multiplication? Could we think we're focused on Jesus and making biblical disciples but actually be focused on making cultural Christians?

What evidence would you put forward to prove your cross hairs are properly calibrated to produce biblical disciples (fully surrendered and willing to pack their bags and *go* like Abraham did)? What contrasting evidence shows your cross hairs are perfectly aligned to something else?

Alan's Insight

"Would you tell me please, which way I ought to go from here?" asked Alice.

"That depends a great deal on where you want to go," said the Cat.

"I don't care where," said Alice.

"Then it doesn't matter which way you walk," said the Cat.

- From Lewis Carroll's *Alice in Wonderland*

Action point #2: As you pursue healthy Kingdom growth, make sure the cross hairs that form and shape your strategies are the right ones. Pause and candidly reflect on the cross hairs that shape and inform your church's strategy. Are they cross hairs that will produce healthy Kingdom growth leading to multiplication? In what ways are the cross hairs perfectly aligned to produce comfortable seekers and safe environments for cultural Christians?

The Cross Hairs of Healthy Kingdom Growth

Let's assume we're putting Jesus at the center and seeking to produce biblical disciples who can and will fuel movements. That's a huge assumption, but necessary for pressing into a framework for healthy Kingdom growth.

The section below provides an overview of four key elements of healthy Kingdom growth. Think of each element as one of four cross hair segments inside our unique scope.

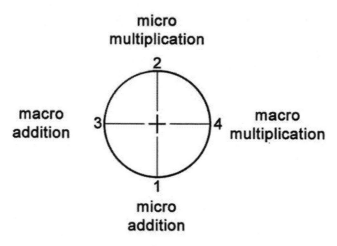

micro
multiplication

macro
addition

macro
multiplication

micro
addition

Consistent with the micro/macro language introduced in *Spark*, these four key elements include: (1) micro-addition, (2) micro-multiplication, (3) macro-addition, and (4) macro-multiplication.

Notice how addition is an essential and vital element to healthy growth, both at the micro and macro level. We need addition *and* multiplication, and we need both the micro (the next one) and the macro (the support and structure to make many).

In our prevailing addition growth-focused cultures, we're missing the multiplication cross hairs. Functionally, we've replaced them with the activities and strategies characteristic of macro-addition. When we shift our target from making biblical disciples to adding numbers, the strategies that grow larger churches (e.g., buildings, new services, new sites, programs, etc.) functionally become our four cross hairs rather than just one of the four.

Consequently, we are left out of balance. Our addition cross hairs will not consistently produce multiplication, and we will be left with the gap between our multiplication aspirations and our actual behaviors. To put it another way, our cross hairs are perfectly aligned to give us the addition-growth, multiplication-muted results we see.

Lets take a deeper look at each of the four elements and how they should function.

Cross Hair #1 – Micro-addition

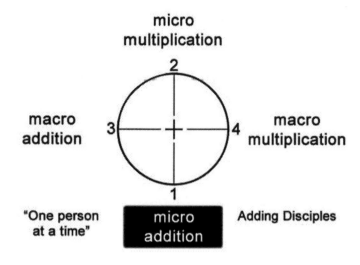

Regardless of our specific strategies, models and approaches, people are added to the movement of Christianity one follower at a time. We can't change that, nor should we try. It's how our Founder designed it to be. Addition is integrally embedded in the core operating system of Christianity.

However, we do need to make a distinction between the process of adding disciples or infants in Christ (cross hair #1) and the process of making or maturing disciples who are fully devoted and surrendered followers of Christ (cross hair #2). While you may prefer to call cross hair #1 "evangelism" (and all its different forms), this framework defines cross hairs #1 and #2 together as biblical discipleship: disciples who make disciples who make disciples.

Infants in the faith spiritually mature and then reproduce themselves repeating the cycle over and over again. The adding and the making *should be* inseparable. Unfortunately, cultural Christianity breaks the reproduction cycle because infants never fully mature and reproduce. To compensate, we wind up doubling down on our macro-addition strategies (e.g., marketing, outreach, programs, etc.).

The pathways for adding disciples—connecting with people, introducing them to Jesus, and bringing them to a point of accepting Him as Lord—are the entry point to making biblical disciples.

Look at Peter's progression. Jesus first said to Peter, "come and see" a *full year* before He called Peter to "follow Me." Then three more years passed before His call to Peter to "die for Me." Clearly, Jesus' command to, "go and make disciples, teaching them to obey all that I have commanded," goes far beyond getting people to a point of accepting Jesus.

In the Bible discipleship is largely a group activity and not just one-on-one personal coaching. Jesus relates to groups of 3-7-12-40-70 respectively. We just do not see Him doing the one-on-one form that we take as standard. It is this ratio that makes discipleship a key ingredient of multiplication.

Alan's Insight

What would have happened if Jesus had left Peter to fend for himself after that initial call to "come and see?" Would he still have developed into the same biblical disciple, or would he have been like the majority of people who heard Jesus' amazing teaching and observed His miracles yet never surrendered to His Lordship?

Our point of decision is not simply to salvation, but rather to life in God's kingdom and discipleship. Stated differently, true faith necessitates repentance and a new journey whereby we seek to live a Kingdom lifestyle and become more like Jesus. Grace and conversion in the Bible lead us to become Jesus' disciples.

Conversion is to enter into the discipleship journey, which continues the throughout the rest of our lives. It's a journey that in its full maturity, and even before then, will lead us to GO. The more we become like the ONE who came to "seek and save the lost," the more we too embrace his kingdom mission and we GO. We go to our neighbors. We go to friends. We go to our family. We go to our co-workers. We carry the fullness of Jesus into our community, our city, our nation, and the world. His commission is an expression of his love. Converts are disciples who are captured by his love and when we finally get what that really means, then WE TOO MUST GO!

The simple graphic below illustrates the need to connect with spiritual seekers regardless of our micro and macro strategies. We must then help bring them to a point of repentance and a decision to accept Jesus as their Lord and Savior, and a commitment to the journey of becoming more like him through a discipleship lifestyle. That is the focus of cross hair #1.

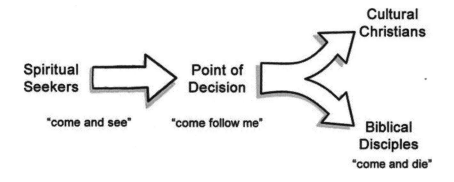

But we can't stop with prayer and confession. The danger and real consequence of focusing 99 percent of our efforts on getting people to the point of saying a prayer (cross hair #1) without a commitment to biblical discipleship, and then only 1 percent on making them into biblical disciples (cross hair #2) is that we produce an army of cultural Christians who are ill-equipped to carry out the Great Commission and make disciples.

Alan's Insight — If we don't disciple people into Jesus' lifestyle, we'll undermine everything else we seek to do. If we fail here, we fail everywhere. Because discipleship is the process of ever-integrating Jesus into the life of the church and then into the world, a church without discipleship is unlikely to produce Christlike followers.

It would be like the 12 disciples spending 99 percent of their effort on marketing, promotion, and advertising to get people out to hear Jesus speak during the feeding of the 5,000, but then leaving them alone to figure out what to do with what they had heard. Think about the crowds that followed Jesus and the disciples. There were actually lots of spiritual seekers and cultural Christians among them. At least until Jesus' teaching got too hard for them. Then they stopped following.

Just maybe our environments and teaching are too safe for those professing faith in Jesus.

Recall that the target we define determines the quality of the movement we get. If we set our standard at accumulating large numbers of spiritual seekers and cultural Christians without equal diligence to make biblical disciples, we will be disappointed in our lack of multiplication.

So how should we add? We can and should do a wide range of things, including one-on-one relationships, outreach events, programs, strong biblical teaching, etc. Ideally, our primary form of micro-addition should be disciples who make disciples, with the church in a supporting role through preaching, programs, ministries, marketing, outreach events, etc.

The healthiest pathway to multiplication is *disciples making disciples* versus *churches making disciples*. We get in trouble when our macro-addition activities become our primary strategies for adding disciples rather than the micro-addition strategy that's part of the master operating system handed down from our Founder.

Alan's Insight   If church attendance, good sermons, and Bible study could produce a movement of disciples, they would have done so by now. Enlist and empower every believer to make disciples. Jesus' Great Commission will never be carried out through the official organization of the church alone.

Truth #3: Micro-addition—adding disciples one at a time—is the strategy embedded in the operating system of Christianity. The best pathway to a multiplication culture is built on the foundation of disciples who mature and make additional disciples. The church's role in macro-addition activities is to support the heavy lifting in the process of disciples making disciples.

Checkpoint #3: Reflect on the "average" or most prevalent pathway to adding new disciples in your church, network or denomination. Is the normal pathway for disciples to make disciples, with the church in a supporting role? Or is the most common pathway for the church to make disciples, with your members inviting their friends to church? Is your primary pathway to disciple making a micro-addition strategy focused on helping individuals make disciples? Or a macro-addition strategy focused on the church attracting spiritual seekers and potential converts?

Action point #3: Ask yourself and your team: In what ways does our current pathway to adding disciples limit or inhibit multiplication? Are we calling people to a serious commitment and surrender to a lifestyle of discipleship that puts them on the path to becoming more fully devoted followers of Jesus? What adjustments are needed?

Multiplication occurs when we see disciples making disciples who make disciples. This requires us to be as intentional in making biblical disciples as we are in making converts.

In all movements, attention must be paid to the core messages of the movement and how these messages can be faithfully maintained as the movement grows. A primary commitment to discipleship and disciple making is a non-negotiable element of all movements that change the world. Factoring in this commitment from the very beginning (in the core DNA) is much easier to do than trying to add it in later on. But regardless, there is no way around the need for discipleship and disciple making.

Alan's Insight

Cross Hair #2 – Micro-multiplication

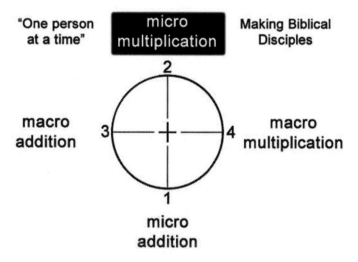

Like micro addition, the "micro" in multiplication is lived out one person at a time. As highlighted above, micro-multiplication occurs when biblical disciples live out their faith by making other

54

disciples. Micro-multiplication is the fuel behind Christian movements.

Alan's Insight

Don't forget that although each new believer is added to the Kingdom one person at a time, the process of making disciples requires that a given disciple should be discipling a few others along the way. In this sense, Christianity is a pay-it-forward movement....it advances exponentially.

A normal part of the maturing process of a biblical disciple is to make other disciples: One becomes many. Recall from our discussion of micro-addition that this is the best possible way to add. Make one biblical disciple and get many more. They reproduce.

Contrast that with cultural Christians. They consume. Add one and continue having to feed them to keep them happy. The insanity occurs when we double our efforts to keep adding more to increase our numbers. As we look for new and innovative ways to use our macro-addition strategies (cross hair #3) to add more people, we spend increasing amounts of time caring for and feeding what we've already accumulated in our coffers.

Alan's Insight

The medium is the message: If you want to use clever and entertaining strategies in mass evangelism, be prepared. You'll create unintended dependencies in the people you win through those methods. It's that darn law of unintended consequences again! What you win them with, you win them to. When you rely on marketing and branding, you set an "entertainment" standard you have to live up to each time. And watch out when a sexier, more attractional church moves in! Disciple making might not be a short-term solution to church growth, but without it your church is doomed to perpetuate merely subtractional and additional cultures.

In micro-addition (cross hair #1) we *add* spiritual infants to our numbers. In micro-multiplication, we *make* either biblical disciples or cultural Christians. We will make one or the other, and both will scale and amplify our efforts—thus they're both categorized as "multiplication."

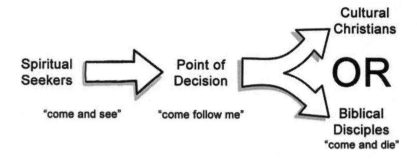

By making biblical disciples, we become more effective at carrying the fullness of Jesus into every corner of our communities and ultimately sending people to *go* and multiply new churches (cross hair #4) that create even greater capacity for healthy Kingdom growth.

Making cultural Christians also scales our efforts ... unfortunately with sideways energy that shunts our multiplication capacity. The more we accumulate spiritual infants who never mature, the more energy we spend running a spiritual nursery to make our infants comfortable and tend to their needs. We need to shift our primary focus from *adding* followers with little emphasis on *making* disciples to a more balanced approach to *adding* and *making* biblical disciples.

We must also cast a vision and have a strategy for continually calling biblical disciples to *go* and plant new communities of faith (cross hair #4). Micro-multiplication is our best fuel for macro-multiplication. Unfortunately, cultural Christians don't respond well to *go*. Our ability to make biblical disciples is the core ingredient needed for macro-multiplication (discussed in the next section).

Bottom line: We need to spend less time and effort figuring out how to get cultural Christians to stay and more time and energy making disciples who will *go*!

Alan's Insight

Leaders in multiplication movements need to be very clear about the definitions, as well as the processes, they use to ensure they actually develop disciples that go. It will not happen by itself! The non-discipling inertia is too engrained into our current system. Multiplying leaders design processes that lock discipleship (becoming like Jesus) and disciple making (methods to ensure discipleship is happening) into the core functions of the church. It's not negotiable!

Truth #4: We will lead our churches to either make cultural Christians or to make biblical disciples. Either way, the impact will multiply our efforts. We will see an expanding number of disciples making disciples with increasing numbers being sent to plant churches, *or* we will see a growing pool of cultural Christians needing our constant care and feeding to keep them happy.

Checkpoint #4: The fruit of a healthy micro-multiplication cross hair is a continual string of leaders sent to start new communities of faith. Is your normal discipleship pathway continually making and preparing biblical disciples to *go*? Are you actively and visibly challenging these disciples to *go*?

Action point #4: Gather your team and look at what your current scorecard results say about the status of cultural Christians vs. biblical disciples being produced at and through your church? Identify the adjustments necessary to seeing a more balanced approach to making biblical disciples. Consider downloading the FREE eBook "Discipleship Handbook" from discipleship.org. This is an excellent resource for assessing how you are doing on seven key elements of a discipleship lifestyle.

Before we move on to look at the macro cross hairs, let's look one more time at the underlying purpose of our vertical cross hair (elements #1 and #2).

Cross Hairs #1 and #2: micro-addition + micro-multiplication = making biblical disciples.

The Discipleship Cross Hairs
micro addition + micro multiplication

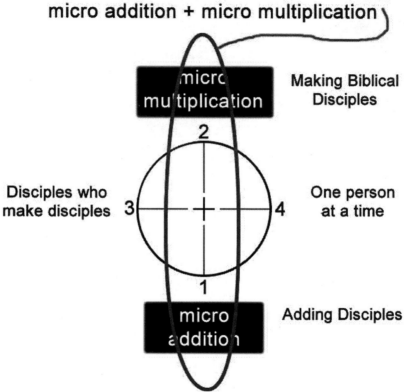

Making Biblical Disciples

Disciples who make disciples

One person at a time

Adding Disciples

Cross Hair #3 – Macro-addition

In our context, "macro" means "capacity" or "capacity building." For our purposes, we're defining capacity as the maximum amount, or number of something, that can function to do what it is designed or intended to do.

So "macro-addition" means to increase our capacity in order to add the way we're designed or intended to add. Where the vertical cross hair (elements #1 and #2) define the core mission of what we're made to do (adding and making biblical disciples), the horizontal cross hair (elements #3 and #4) are about adding and building capacity to make biblical disciples.

Vertical cross hair = DISCIPLESHIP.

Horizontal cross hair = CAPACITY.

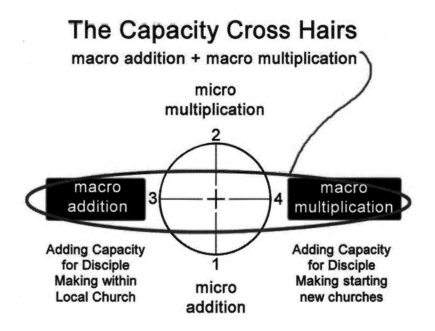

The Capacity Cross Hairs
macro addition + macro multiplication

micro multiplication

2

macro addition **3** **4** macro multiplication

Adding Capacity for Disciple Making within Local Church

1

micro addition

Adding Capacity for Disciple Making starting new churches

Think about a small business owner. Maybe a sole proprietor who runs a carpet-cleaning business. One van. One employee. Working from home. Supplies stored in the garage. Capacity is limited to what this one person with one van can execute. Unfortunately, every minute he's out at a specific job is a minute he's not generating new business or building new capacity for expanding the company.

To grow, he must add employees, vans and equipment. Eventually, he will need a facility to truly scale up. The institutional part of the business, including its infrastructure, processes and resources, is vital to multiplying the growth of the business. To grow the business, the owner must increasingly pay attention to his capacity for growth.

The need to build capacity into the system requires that we have a different paradigm of the church - a paradigm able to legitimize new priorities and behaviors. Becoming part of a movement will affect everything: vision, strategy, budgeting, and priorities. Your current budgeting will highlight what your church takes seriously. If most of your budget goes to weekend programming, that's a pretty good clue to what your priorities are and what you value. The budget is a theological document!

Alan's Insight

In His wisdom, God gave us the church—in part because we are designed to function like a family, and also to provide us a platform of capacity for (1) increasing our effectiveness in disciple making and (2) scaling or multiplying our efforts at disciple making (beyond what unaffiliated, lone ranger disciples can do when they're separated from biblical fellowship).

Micro-addition happens in the local church, functioning as a family, and creating processes, structures, ministries, and other elements of capacity to increase our ability to make biblical disciples. We add capacity for micro-addition at the local church level. It's the scope of things under the authority of the local church leadership.

Think of all the activities a local church can do to create local capacity for adding numbers (regardless of the activity's effectiveness at producing biblical disciples). This list includes but isn't limited to:

- New worship services (including online services and services with different music styles, times and locations)
- New facilities
- New sites or campuses

- New staff
- New programs and ministries
- New partnerships
- New churchwide campaigns
- Marketing (e.g., direct mail campaigns, signs, banners, online advertising, social media, etc.)
- Outreach events
- Small groups and Bible studies
- Leadership development and training
- Missional communities

Yes, local capacity is vital to healthy growth. The Acts 2 church illustrates that point. Because of the church's macro-addition elements and activities, the church had more capacity for growth. Look at the collective "they" statements we find in Acts 2:46-47:

They met daily.
They broke bread together.
They had everything in common.
They sold property and possessions to give to those in need.

The last part of verse 47 tells us: "and God added to their number daily those who were being saved." We see corporate behaviors leading to personal salvations. But it was what individuals were doing together, to and for each other, and not what the institution was doing to or for its members. *They* activities are at the heart of corporate macro-addition capacity. This macro-addition capacity creates context for micro-addition and multiplication.

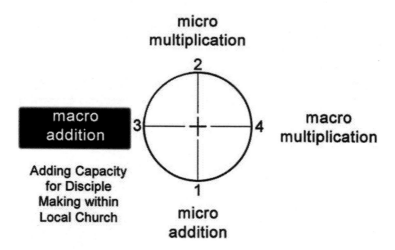

micro
multiplication

macro
addition

macro
multiplication

Adding Capacity
for Disciple
Making within
Local Church

micro
addition

Look back at the *they* list above. Think about the specific activities and why the Acts 2 church did them. Now, critically ask yourself, *Why are we doing the things we are doing?* Is it to experience the *they* practices of the early church—the practices and behaviors that lead to making disciples? Or is it primarily motivated by corporate efforts to produce increased attendance? It's vital that we see the early Christians' pattern of disciple making. For them, their *they* macro-addition behaviors led to more effective micro efforts to make disciples. The fruitfulness came in God adding to their numbers. We see the early church focused on *they* behaviors and reliant on God to produce the growth. This is in contrast to our macro-addition corporate strategies that are primarily aimed at attendance growth rather than supporting micro-addition and multiplication.

Possibly the single-largest obstacle to multiplication occurs when we position macro-addition activities as our primary strategy for growth, rather than seeing these activities as a supporting element to micro-addition and multiplication. Too many churches have unintentionally put macro-addition strategies and goals as the target of their cross hairs.

The result? Though we increase our effectiveness at breaking organizational growth barriers and adding to our numbers, unfortunately we may be building bigger and bigger holding tanks for cultural Christians.

Why aren't we seeing multiplication? Because we're perfectly aligned to get what we're putting at the intersection of our cross hairs!

Truth #5: Macro-addition is about adding local capacity for making biblical disciples. It's intended to support and enhance the efforts of disciples making disciples. Too often, we substitute the capacity-building activities of macro-addition into the bull's-eye of our cross hairs. We end up shunting multiplication by producing cultural Christians rather than biblical disciples.

Checkpoint #5: In what ways have you relied on macro-addition strategies for growth rather than using them to enhance micro-addition and multiplication for making biblical disciples?

Action point #5: Reread this section and then make a list of adjustments (in your thinking and your strategy) to help you properly position and see macro-addition activities as supporting elements rather than core elements for making disciples.

Cross Hair #4 – Macro-multiplication

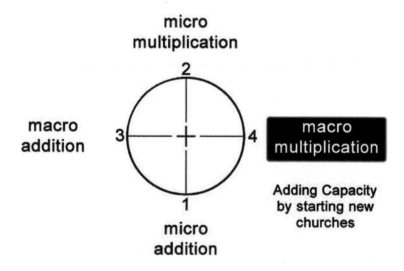

63

Macro-addition is needed, but it *is not* the most leveraged form of capacity building. Again, where macro-addition focuses on increasing the capacity to grow trees in our own orchard, macro-multiplication focuses on planting new orchards. We need both.

Macro-multiplication creates Kingdom capacity for implementing new environments and contexts for biblical disciple making. This key element requires that we release and send leaders, dollars and support to be used in starting new communities of faith that are not directly under our control and authority.

This is not an issue of choosing one over the other. It's healthy local capacity from which we develop and deploy leaders to start new churches. Healthy macro-multiplication is enhanced by macro-addition systems and activities. For example, the same leadership development systems that support local church capacity expansion can be used for developing and deploying church planters.

Letting go of our macro-addition scorecards takes courageous leadership. Recall the behaviors reflected in the Multiplication Quiz at the beginning of this book. A church committed to macro-multiplication will demonstrate the following types of behaviors:

- Multiplying churches have a scorecard that is as focused on starting new churches as it is adding new members.

- Multiplying churches give their first fruits to church planting, including at least the first 10 percent of their tithes and offerings.

- Multiplying churches have a specific vision and strategy for multiplication, including accountability measures for monitoring progress.

- Multiplying churches value raising up and deploying leaders to plant churches. This includes an intern/residency program for developing and deploying church planting leaders and team members.

- Multiplying churches send church planters on an ongoing and regular basis to plant new churches.

- Multiplying churches value new churches over mortgage debt. They plant their first church before taking on mortgage debt, and they commit additional financial resources (beyond a tithe) as a percentage of mortgage debt (taking on new mortgage debt is matched by committing a higher percentage of the budget to church planting). Multiplying churches take proactive actions to ensure mortgage debt will not constrain church planting support.

- Multiplying churches value new churches over new sites. They plant their first church before adding their first site. They commit to plant five-plus churches for each new site they add. Multiplying churches understand that multi-site is a macro-addition strategy than can adversely impact macro-multiplication strategies.

- Multiplying churches value "sending" staff and leaders to plant churches. They send their first planter before accumulating their first three staff members and continue to send a percentage of staff members to plant churches.

- Multiplying churches inspire, encourage, and challenge church members to participate in church planting, both financially and by being part of church planting teams. Multiplying churches continually affirm those who *go*.

These are tough practices, but necessary if we are to be multiplying churches who value multiplication.

Alan's Insight

What you measure improves and what you celebrate gets repeated. It is vital to reinforce the behavior you want repeated. Keep score and measure performance to determine consistency with values. Tangibly and intangibly recognize performance that's consistent with espoused values. Simply measuring performance often improves it. But rewards and recognition will reinforce values as well. The important message to keep in mind is that what you choose to reinforce is what people will choose to value.

Truth #6: Macro-multiplication is about adding Kingdom capacity for making biblical disciples beyond our local church. Most of the behavioral characteristics of multiplying churches require that we move beyond an adding-accumulating focus to a releasing-sending focus. The scorecards of multiplying churches are rooted in deploying rather than accumulating.

Checkpoint #6: In what ways does your church's scorecard reflect macro-multiplication? Macro-addition? Are these two dimensions balanced? Do your macro-addition strategies enhance and expand your macro-multiplication activity?

Action point #6: Take the time to sit down with your team and go through this section. What adjustments are needed to create a more balanced scorecard that includes multiplication?

Reproducing in Every Direction

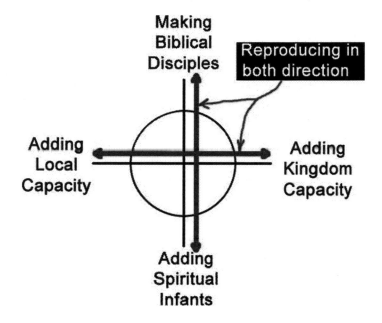

At the core of healthy Kingdom growth is reproduction. Disciples making disciples who make disciples in the vertical cross hair. As disciples become more like Jesus with His fullness in them, they carry that fullness to others and help bring new spiritual infants into the family. The process repeats and fuels itself. Biblical disciples reproduce while cultural Christians consume, and thus we see the importance of putting biblical disciples as the target of our cross hairs.

Healthy growth also involves reproduction in the horizontal cross hair. Capacity must be reproduced. Locally, we grow our capacity by reproducing internally. This expanding capacity supports the discipleship efforts of the vertical cross hairs. Globally, we grow by reproducing our local capacity into new autonomous churches and sending/deploying biblical disciples. These new churches then repeat the process. Multiplication is suppressed when we focus 99 percent of our effort on local capacity (macro-addition).

Raising the Bar

Alan's Insight

Movement leader Neil Cole has famously stated that we should raise the bar on discipleship and lower the bar on how church is done. There is a huge amount of movemental punch in this statement. If we make discipleship non-negotiable and church much easier to reproduce, then we prime the system for movement. Shifting strategy to accomplish this will, over time, make a huge amount of difference in any church or organization.

As you pursue healthy Kingdom growth, you have the opportunity to raise the bar in your church on what it means to follow Jesus. Instead of creating cultural Christians, what would it look like to birth new Christians who grew in their faith? What would it look like in your church and the world at large if we were producing modern-day disciples—those who were so devoted to Jesus that they left their ordinary lives to follow Him and eventually died for spreading the gospel?

We can't help but think that our churches and our world would look tremendously different if the disciples we made actually took the Great Commission to head and heart. It's up to courageous leaders like you who will embrace values and strategies that produce these kinds of followers, and then equip, challenge and release them to go.

In the next chapter, you'll get the information you need to start to discern where your church is on the multiplication scale and more importantly, what it will take to become a Level 5 multiplying church that raises the bar.

Chapter 3
Rethinking Multiplication

Though you may not think about it, your experience es with the individuals in the various contexts of your life—home, work, school, church, etc.—cause us to naturally group people into profiles. For example, after one meeting, a small group leader knows who the "extra grace required" (EGR) people are in the group, the ones who dominate the conversation. If you're a teacher, within the first week of school you know who the over-achievers are. And if you are or have ever been a supervisor or manager, you quickly learn who to turn to when something vitally important needs to be finished with excellence.

Reputations are built on demonstrated behaviors and results. In each of the above examples, you could observe the behaviors of a specific group and then create profiles based on their behaviors. In other words, you could study the characteristics of "extra grace required" people and then define a profile for that type of person based on their demonstrated behaviors. Anyone in a small group could read the profile and say, "Sure enough, Brian was an EGR in the group I was in last year!"

The DISC behavioral assessment offers a great example of profiling personality types. After taking the DISC assessment, participants receive a personalized report that defines in detail four profile types: D, I, S, and C. Most of us could skip taking the test and discern our personality type simply by reading the profile descriptions.

In this chapter, we're introducing behavioral types that describe five different levels of multiplication in churches. We define these as Level 1, 2, 3, 4, and 5 multiplying churches. Regardless of church size, growth rate (positive or negative), or profile type, all churches will exhibit behaviors from all of these five levels. We can create profiles for each of the five behavioral types.

As you may have guessed, Level 5 churches are the most aggressive multiplying churches, and Level 1 churches are the least. Where DISC profiles aggregate a person's behaviors from all four primary personality types into a primary type, churches can also demonstrate behaviors from more than one multiplying profile, yet can still be assigned to a single most prominent type.

You might be surprised to learn that most of the largest and fastest-growing churches that make our "envy lists" are actually Level 3 multiplying churches. For this framework, we've intentionally defined churches with a strong addition-growth culture yet are not aggressively multiplying, as Level 3 churches.

Alan's Insight

Our definition of success seldom reaches beyond what we call addition-growth churches. This is important because as we've already learned, we generally get what we are aiming for. If all of our exemplary churches are Level 3, then our standards of success are in fact limiting our missional potential. We need to think much bigger, and reach much higher, than we currently are doing.

If we are to move the needle on multiplication, we must start by creating a new scorecard. After all, who wants to aspire to be a Level 3 church when you could be a Level 5 church? (And make no mistake—your church was made to be a Level 5!)

Do you recall our earlier discussion about the gap between a church's aspirations and behaviors? This gap is caused when our macro-addition strategies and focus overpower and take the place of macro-multiplication. Believe it or not, many Level 3 churches are actually stuck, even though their accumulation statistics look good. The very macro strategies that propelled them to Level 3 are the same ones that are keeping them from becoming a Level 4 or 5 multiplying church.

At Exponential, we continue to hear from senior pastors who have started and grown large churches to Level 3. They're wondering if there just might be something more. Many are even experiencing discontent that's awakening them to something beyond a macro-addition focus. Clearly, the gap between their Level 3 reality and the Level 5 their church was designed for will always cause discontent.

At this point, you might be saying, "I only *wish* our church was a Level 3. Then we'd then have the resources to multiply." The truth is that most new churches are born into Level 1; 80 percent to 90 percent of churches in the U.S. are a Level 1 or 2. If that's your church, don't let this truth paralyze you. In fact, count your blessings. The reality is that this elusive, tension-free day when churches can afford to multiply will never come, even for Level 3 churches. They are stuck for a reason.

If you're leading a Level 1 or 2 church, we want you to hear this: *The behaviors, values, and decisions you make now position you to become a future Level 4 or 5 multiplying church,* possibly even bypassing some of the limitations Level 3 churches experience.

Alan's Insight What a church becomes is directly related to both the direction, as well as the quality, of the choices you make now. In a very real sense, your church is perfectly designed to achieve what you're currently achieving. So if you're in decline or plateaued, look for the factors that are biasing you toward those outcomes. Take charge of your design! A redesign at the levels of vision, strategy, and culture will determine your church's future viability. Multiplication is all in the design!

Plain and simple, setting your sights on Level 3 as your definition of success is a futile exercise. You'll eventually find yourself feeling empty and, like many leaders today, wondering if there's something more. *How might things be different if you reworked your scorecard for success and embraced the practices and behaviors of Level 5 multiplying churches?*

Regardless of the level you find yourself at today, the key is to consider where you are, where you'd like to go, and what you need to change today to move yourself in the right direction.

With this book and our 2016 "Becoming Five" theme, Exponential has worked to:
• create a new vocabulary and scorecard for multiplication;
• give you a tool to discern where you are today;
• present a framework for where you can go tomorrow;
• call churches to a future beyond addition growth.

Integrating the Micro and Macro

In chapter 2, we talked about healthy Kingdom growth. Our targeting scope for multiplication must have its sights set to:

- the right target: making biblical disciples of Jesus (versus adding cultural Christians);

- the right vertical cross hairs: *Disciple Making*. Adding spiritual infants with micro-addition and making biblical disciples with micro-multiplication. Micro-addition + micro-multiplication = biblical disciple making;

- the right horizontal cross hairs: *Capacity*. Adding local capacity within the local church to support disciple making, and adding global or Kingdom capacity by sending people to plant new churches;

- practices and behaviors that balance the four dimensions and keep our scorecards focused on biblical disciple making. Disciples that make disciples who make disciples with a bias to *go*.

Our approach to building profiles for the five levels of multiplying churches has a strong bias to behaviors and results. We focus primarily on the horizontal cross hairs of capacity, understanding that the quality of disciple making is what will fuel (or limit) the potential level of multiplication at any of the five levels.

Consider these three examples focusing on Level 1, 3 and 5 churches:

- A Level 1 church struggling to survive in its context might be making biblical disciples. But because of a lack of vision, strategy, and leadership within the church, those disciples are never encouraged and challenged to *go* even though the natural impulse for biblical disciples is to *go*. Because the leadership lives in the tension of scarcity, they suppress the *go* impulse, not wanting to lose members. In this case, the level of multiplication is not about the quality of disciple making; instead it's a lack of courageous leadership to release others.

- A large, growing Level 3 church is internally reproducing but is only sending by accident when someone decides to *go*. The church may be doing a poor job at producing biblical disciples, yet they are growing and reproducing locally as they add. They will not progress to Level 4 or 5 without improving the quality of disciple making and embracing a value of multiplication that leads to new strategies and new behaviors.

- A Level 5 multiplying church of any type or size simply cannot become Level 5 without both a strong emphasis on biblical disciple making and a value of multiplication that encourages, develops, and releases disciples to *go*.

We need a renewed theological focus on Jesus and the gospel, disciple making, incarnational messaging, leader releasing, multiplication organizing, and risk taking.

Alan's Insight

In all three cases, we have to be careful not to let the quality of disciple making define the level of multiplication and vice versa.

The approach we're taking here is to profile and highlight behaviors at each level, trusting that the quality of discipleship needs to be the target of our cross hairs at all levels of multiplication. In this way, we're focusing and pressing into the behaviors that distinguish macro-addition and macro-multiplication—and the synergistic balance between the two.

Level 5 church leaders simultaneously value biblical disciple making *and* church multiplication. They understand the synergistic relationship between the two and have the courage to demand and resource for both.

Developing the Profiles

In the following section, we work through the foundational elements that shape and define the five profiles of multiplying churches.

In case you're cynical, there is nothing magical or specifically biblical about "five" levels. Others might use six, seven or even 10 levels of multiplication. We've chosen to look at five because they correspond nicely to the way we could naturally segregate the churches in the U.S. into different behavior profiles. Also, "five" is a memorable number that's small enough to maintain simplicity and large enough to make notable distinctions between the levels.

Grouping Churches by Growth Behaviors and Characteristics

Subtracting

Scarcity
Thinking

Subtraction

Let's start with the approximately 80 percent of churches in the U.S. that are subtracting or have plateaued.

The 80 percent stat tells us that the vast majority of churches in the United States exist in a subtraction or survival culture. These Level 1 churches are living in a

74

culture that simply makes it hard for them to even *think* about multiplication. The average church in America plateaus below 100 members and struggles to grow. They are in survival mode, often experiencing subtraction. The lead pastor wants to be full time, and the leader's top stresses are often finances, starting with their own salary. It takes about 100 members to support a full-time pastor in most settings, so there is a constant and real tension on finances. They have a "scarcity" mentality with a perspective of, "We will add [fill in the blank] after we can afford it." Unfortunately, until they grow these churches are caught in the paradox of never being able to afford the things they need to springboard into an addition culture. They are stuck and often struggling to keep their heads above water.

 With the vast majority of churches in North America in long-term, trended, decline, what can we learn by auditing the thinking and behaviors that encode the decline into the organization? We find a different DNA and operating system in these churches than in Level 5 multiplying churches.

Alan's Insight

Adding

16%

Growth
Thinking

Addition

The second culture to consider is addition-growth. Some 15 to 20 percent of U.S churches find themselves here. We've talked extensively in this book and *Spark* about our addiction for addition-growth, rooted in a macro-addition scorecard. These churches are defined as Level 3 multiplying churches.

In addition-growth churches, attendance is increasing. Many are often externally focused, making an impact in their surrounding communities. Many have added multisite venues. In the midst of their growth, key tensions inevitably arise: How do we continue growing? How will we staff the ministries? How will we maintain the weekly production, mortgage and other associated costs of growth?

These churches have come face to face with growth tensions: Should we build? How big? What type? They've hired multiple staff. The pursuit of adding full-time paid staff has firmly established and rooted them in an addition-growth culture. Each new hire helps plug a hole that has limited growth (or positions the church for growth in an untapped area).

A successful Level 3 church is adept at evangelizing the immediate cultural context, but is seldom effective beyond more complex cultural contexts. As such, it picks the low-hanging fruit but lacks a strategy to reach the fruit higher up.

Alan's Insight

These churches are often looked to as the "innovative churches" because they've demonstrated new and creative ways to reach more people and break through growth barriers.

Few of these churches have ever been challenged with, or have even considered, a different paradigm:

- Should we plant our first church before building?
- Should we plant our first church before doing our first site?
- Should we add a church planting intern/resident before our next staff hire?
- Should we tithe (give our first 10 percent) to church planting?

For these churches, releasing resources to macro-multiplication directly competes with the very resources that fuel their macro-addition strategies. And only one wins out!

These churches are at a crucial point in their development in terms of setting the course of their future relative to addition-growth culture versus multiplication-growth culture. Their choices are numerous "line in the sand" decisions that could shape their core values, convictions and practices. The path for most keeps them

76

captive and stuck, preventing them from moving beyond Level 3 multiplication.

The First Three Levels

Alan's Insight

The concepts of church (ecclesiology) inherited from Europe and the Reformation are innately hard to reproduce and are designed to grow, if at all, by addition. But it's going to take a different approach - what we call movement-thinking and movement-acting - to move towards reproducing (Level 4) and multiplication (Level 5).

We've looked at the first two distinct cultures in churches: Subtraction (scarcity thinking) and Addition (growth thinking). Let's integrate those cultures to show the first levels of multiplying churches, which represent 96 percent of all U.S. churches:

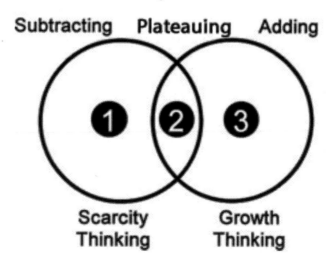

Levels 1, 2 and 3

Subtracting   Plateauing   Adding

1   2   3

Scarcity   Growth
Thinking   Thinking

Plateauing

Note that the subtraction and addition circles overlap with no clear dividing line between a culture of subtraction and a culture of addition. In region 2 on the image above, churches in this area demonstrate some characteristics of both subtraction and addition cultures. Their thinking lies in a state of tension between scarcity and growth.

These churches have survived and may be growing. They have growth in their sights with Level 3 at the pinnacle, but are constrained by their scarcity thinking. Their focus and aspirations center on growth and addition: How do we get to 100? 200? 500? What is our strategy? Do we build or buy? Do we start a new non-profit? Do we hire a family minister? These churches are consumed with identifying the actions that will move them toward Level 3.

They may be experiencing the "silver bullet syndrome" that causes them to look for that one program, activity, or project they believe will propel them into addition-growth. The lure and appeal of graduating to Level 3 addition is very strong and consumes their thinking.

In summary, our first three levels of multiplying churches are:
• Level 1 characterized by subtraction and scarcity thinking
• Level 2 characterized by plateau, survival, and tension between scarcity and growth
• Level 3 characterized by a strong addition-growth culture.

From Chapter 2, we'd say these churches are strongly aligned to a micro- and macro-addition focus.

Let's pause and consider why these first three levels are even considered multiplication. The church, and the biblical disciples that call it home, have the latent capacity to catalyze movements. The apparent health (or lack thereof) of a church says little about the latent capacity waiting to be activated in individual believers.

For example, the church where I (Todd) became a Christian was 20-plus years old and had never run more than approximately 150 people. The church was a strong shepherding and care-taking church without a strong macro-addition or macro-multiplication focus. There was no vision or strategy for church planting. And yet a handful of leaders who made that church their home for a season of time moved on to play a role in starting hundreds of different churches and church planting ministries (including Exponential).

There is a movement waiting to be birthed in the DNA of each believer. The seeds can sprout forth even in spite of a local church's lack of vision for multiplication. Multiplication can be birthed because of, *or* in spite of a local church. As we move from "in spite of" to "because of," we see churches moving from the lower levels of multiplication to Levels 4 and 5. All churches have the capacity and the DNA for multiplication.

Multiplication *Integrating Levels 4 and 5*

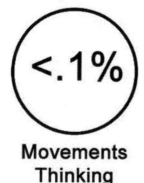

Movements Thinking

Very few U.S. churches experience a multiplication culture. Exponential's dream and prayer is to see an increasing number of churches move into a radically multiplying (or exponential) culture—currently represented by less than .005 percent of U.S. churches. These leaders plant churches as a normal and regular part of their existence. They continually develop and send people to plant. Their

79

scorecard is more about "who and how many have been sent" than "how many have been accumulated." Churches with a multiplication culture have broken free from the bondage of Level 3 macro-addition thinking and have put practices in place that close the gap between multiplication behaviors and aspirations. They are courageous leaders who are more burdened by building Kingdom capacity than local church capacity. These are Level 5 multiplying churches.

 Embracing the movement paradigm requires us to think and act fundamentally different than what the prevailing "non-movemental" forms of church require. While we have the innate capacity for movement, unfortunately most of our thinking and practices are

Alan's Insight non-movemental.

The overlap area between addition and multiplication gives us Level 4, labeled "Reproducing." It's estimated that less than 5 percent of U.S. churches ever reproduce in their lifetime.

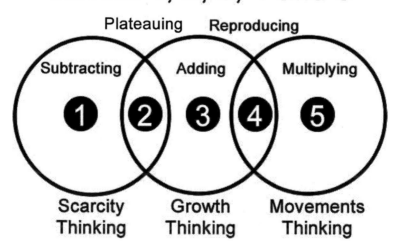

Level 4 leaders sense something new and fresh. Maybe because they've already embraced a different scorecard, or maybe because they simply feel a holy discontent that something needs to change.

These leaders almost instinctively know that more of the same will not get us to where we need to go. They desire and are willing to move to Level 5, and might be making progress, but the tensions and force pulling them back to Level 3 limit their ability to move more fully into region 5.

Here is the paradigm shift that is required for us to think outside the box of traditional models founded on addition-thinking. We need an alternative vision of the church to be able to live into it.

Alan's Insight

In summary, Level 1 churches are subtracting; Level 2 are plateauing; Level 3 are adding; Level 4 are reproducing; and Level 5 are multiplying.

The Appendix at the back of this book includes the more detailed descriptions of the five profiles for multiplying churches.

New Assessment Tool for Measuring Your Multiplication Culture

Exponential has introduced a new Becoming Five assessment tool, which is modeled after the DISC personality profile approach. The tool features the following elements:

- *Profiles* - Each of the five levels of multiplying churches has a description, including characteristic behaviors and practices. The descriptions of the five levels in the above sections are a form of qualitative "profiles." As you read through each description in the Appendix, you will likely find yourself saying, "Yes that sounds like us," or "No, that's not really us," or "Yeah, that kind of sounds like us." Although churches will exhibit characteristics from several different profiles, their aggregated behaviors place them with an average assessment score at either Level 1, 2, 3, 4 or 5.

- **Simple and memorable vocabulary** - The core essence of "Becoming Five," focuses on the pursuit of a new multiplication scorecard, multiplication values, and multiplication behaviors. This is a journey into new territory, one that takes courageous leadership to buck the addition-growth scorecards that are so deeply embedded in our identities.

Together, these elements, along with language, stories, and symbols, form the essence of a multiplying culture. Leaders can change the feel and direction of their church by pursuing these culture-creating values.

Alan's Insight

The profiles are simply "Level 1, 2, 3, 4 and 5 Multiplying Churches"—"sticky" terminology that we believe churches will easily embrace and relate to. It's simple, intuitive, and takes minimal effort to identify and understand where your church is. Finally, we believe the simple vocabulary gives us a more inspiring and biblical goal—beyond the Level 3 scorecards we've adopted. The pursuit of Level 5 gives us a "new normal" to aspire to.

- **Three-dimensional view** - The assessment tool scores churches on three distinct "views" of their multiplication practices: 1) past, 2) present, and 3) future behaviors and results. Each "view" is scored separately based on answers to 20 questions in each of the three views (a total of 60 questions).

- *Multiplying levels* - Churches receive separate scores for each of the three views plus an aggregated score combining all three views. The aggregated score is reported on a five-point scale rounded to the nearest level (e.g., Level 1, 2, 3, 4 or 5).

- *Multiplication patterns* - The three individual scores for a church's past, present and future behaviors form a unique pattern or series of numbers. For example, a 1-1-5 pattern represents a church that has Level 1 behaviors in the past (1) and present (1), but aspires to be a Level 5 church in the coming years (5). Multiplication patterns give us a simple to understand snapshot of where a church has been and where it would like to go.

   Between the patterns 1-1-1 and 5-5-5, there are 125 unique three-digit patterns. However, most all churches will fall into one of seven core patterns of interest. With each of these seven patterns, we've assigned a representative name or term that reflects the pattern characteristics.

   For example, a 1-1-5 is an *aspiring pattern* because it represents a future level that is significantly higher than what the church has demonstrated in the past. A 3-4-5 on the other hand is a *reproducing pattern*, representing steady, enduring progress toward Level 5. The needs of churches in each of the seven patterns are different. Assigning patterns is helpful, as future resources can be developed for each pattern of churches based on the specific challenges within each pattern.

Visit exponential.org and other participating church planting web sites to take the assessment (available late Fall 2015).

Profiles: Five Levels of Multiplying Churches

Read through the descriptions of each profile included in the Appendix. Which characteristics best describe your church?

Key Patterns from the Profiles

Diagnosis is the first step in the development of treatment. We take this as a given when we go to the doctor, but we seldom take the time to diagnose the living systems we call church. Honest self-assessment is very necessary to growth and development. Identifying your church's multiplication profile and pattern is key to developing a forward strategy.

Alan's Insight

As we just explained, the Becoming Five assessment looks at three different lenses or views: past, present, and future. Each lens is scored relative to the five levels of multiplication we've put forth, and a unique three-digit score or pattern is assigned (e.g. 1-1-5).

There are 125 different possible patterns between 1-1-1 and 5-5-5. However, many of these patterns such as 5-1-1 are meaningless and are not included in the core patterns. Additionally, many numbers can be grouped together into a common pattern. For example, a 1-2-4 and a 1-2-5 are essentially the same pattern.

The net result is seven key or core patterns that most churches will test into. These core patterns include:

- *Aspiring pattern* (e.g., 1-1-4, 1-1-5, 1-2-4, 1-2-5, 2-2-4, and 2-2-5)
- *Advancing pattern* (e.g., 1-3-4, 1-3-5, 2-3-4, and 2-3-5)
- *Breakout pattern* (e.g., 3-3-4 and 3-3-5)
- *Reproducing pattern* (e.g., 3-4-4 and 3-4-5)
- *Addition pattern* (any pattern ending in 3)
- *Survivor pattern* (any pattern ending in 1 or 2)
- *Recovery pattern* (any pattern dropping from past to present and then increasing in the future view to 4 or 5)

The pattern assignments are simply a tool for giving churches a snapshot of where they've been, where they are, and where they'd like to go. As you carefully look at the differences in each of the seven patterns, you'll see unique challenges and issues for each unique pattern. Our hope is that this framework will help create a new vocabulary, as well as new resources, to equip churches to move beyond Level 3 to become Level 4 and 5 multiplying churches.

Moving Forward

Putting a critical eye on our weaknesses and shortcomings is never easy. However, if we are to be courageous leaders who take the actions needed to close the gap between our multiplication behaviors and aspirations, we must start by looking candidly at how we are doing.

"The illiterate of the 21st century will not be those who cannot read and write, but those who cannot learn, unlearn, and relearn."- Alvin Toffler

Alan's Insight

Half the battle is acknowledging our weakness; handing our shortcomings over to God; and prayerfully and sincerely asking Him to birth a passion in us for multiplication—a passion that spills over into the decisions we make and the practices we put in place.

We encourage you to discover your multiplication number (i.e., the level your church is multiplying at) and your multiplication pattern. Maybe you've identified your numbers by simply reading the descriptions in this chapter. If not, consider taking the Becoming Five assessment at exponential.org (or other participating church planting web sites featuring the Becoming Five logo).

After discovering your numbers, consider taking the following action steps to develop a multiplication strategy:

- Commit to develop a written multiplication plan;
- Prayerfully listen for God's whisper and leading;
- Consider forming a team within your church to perform a more detailed internal review/assessment of your growth culture. Then consider using the 60 questions of the Becoming Five assessment as a basis for your detailed assessment. Identify the changes you need to make over the next five years to move you closer to Level 5. Then prioritize those changes and take one step at a time, acknowledging that the process will take several years;
- In coming years, take advantage of Becoming Five resources developed by Exponential and other organizations for each of the seven core multiplication patterns.
- Search for and identify like-minded leaders at other churches who are burdened by multiplication and then journey together to learn and hold one another accountable.
- Join or affiliate with a denomination or group that can provide direct support to enhance your journey.

Becoming a Level 5 multiplying church isn't likely to happen on your own. You need coaching, training, consulting, peer-to-peer accountability, etc. Also vital - find a peer group that legitimizes your journey, facilitates peer learning, and shares best practices.

Alan's Insight

Be courageous leaders that are prepared for tension, but willing to pay the price for a better future!

Chapter 4
Embracing Tension

Have you ever thought that tension in life begins the moment we take our first breath—the very minute we come into this world as screaming babies? Jesus promised it. He told His disciples, "In this world, you will have trouble" (John 16:33). It's not simply an option or possibility. Tension in our lives is unavoidable.

You probably know that churches aren't immune to trouble. And we don't have to tell you that churches also live in a constant state of tension. As a key element of Jesus' strategy against Satan, why would we expect anything less? Regardless of whether a church is a Level 1 or Level 5 or somewhere in between, the tensions it experiences can distract and keep it from being and becoming what the Founder intends.

That doesn't change the fact that we try as hard as we can to avoid tension, conquer it, or make it go away.

Don't miss this important truth: *No matter what level of multiplication you find yourself at, you will have tension.* Nothing you do will allow you to reach a level of multiplication that is tension-free. The Level 1 church that lives in a scarcity culture will not suddenly find itself tension-free when it graduates to a Level 3 church. The tensions will simply shift to new ones.

Hopefully, the problems brought about by natural growth will produce healthy responses in the host organization. In other words, multiplication can create a tension that forces us to find better solutions and to be better people. It's a problem for sure, but a good one to have.

Alan's Insight

So the key questions for you and your church are not, "Will we have tension?" or "How do we avoid tension?" The game changer is how you leverage tension to grow and more deeply embed a culture of multiplication in your DNA. The profound, transformative question is always, "How do we leverage the behaviors of multiplying churches to help us maneuver and grow in this current season of tension?"

In other words, regardless of what your current level of multiplication actually is, you must make an intentional decision to act and behave like a multiplying church (Level 5). Think of a specific tension you're currently dealing with in your church and ask yourself: *What would it look like to respond to this tension the way a multiplying church would respond?*

 Alan's Insight To properly assess your current system, you have to have an alternative vision of the church than the one we currently have. You can't measure growth against the prevailing model, but only in light of the church as missional movement.

That is what courageous leaders who value multiplication do. They lean into the future and create a new normal; they defy the status quo for the context they currently find themselves in.

Tensions are Like Strong Magnets (or Springs)

Recall our integrated picture of the cultures that are core to our five levels of multiplication:

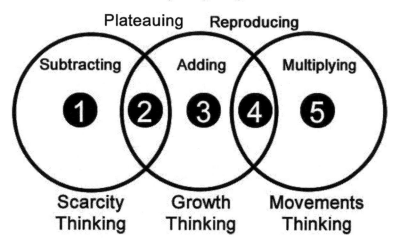

Now, consider what would happen if we placed a strong magnet to the left of Level 1. For this illustration, assume your church is now a metal object in the Level 1 circle.

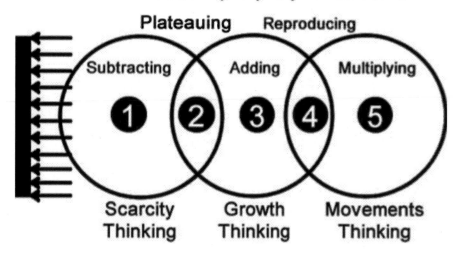

Now think about a magnet. The closer you get to it, the stronger its attractive force. When you're a foot away, you don't even feel its force. The diagram above shows that the farther you move to the right (toward Level 2 and higher), the less you feel the subtraction magnet. Here's the corollary: The closer you get to a magnet's force field, the stronger the force and the tougher it becomes to ever break free of its grip.

Many of the practices we still use are now obsolete because they were formed in completely different cultural conditions. When we learn the art of movement-thinking, we begin to recognize that the church is responsible for delivering the message of Jesus in radically different and constantly changing cultural conditions - requiring movement and constant adaptation.

Alan's Insight

In this illustration, the force field near the magnet represents the culture you create in your church. If you create a survival culture, you'll constantly experience the tension of scarcity drawing you toward subtraction.

Those churches that do break free to Level 2 begin to experience the force field of the addition magnet (see the next graphic).

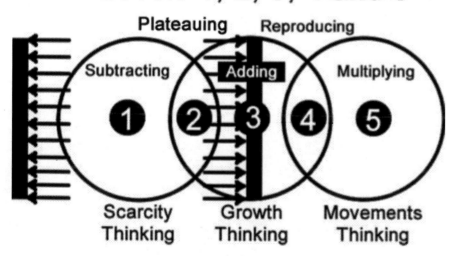

Levels 1, 2, 3, 4 and 5

Plateauing   Reproducing

Subtracting   Adding   Multiplying

① ② ③ ④ ⑤

Scarcity   Growth   Movements
Thinking   Thinking   Thinking

In addition-growth culture, the addition magnet is very strong. As a church moves toward it, the magnet's force becomes increasingly powerful and even addictive. We've described the journey in Level 3 as the continuing process of conquering the next growth barrier. This Level 3 magnet is at the center of addition-growth, drawing your church closer and closer.

The church in the Level 2 region feels the effects of both the subtraction and the addition magnets.

For example, a church growing toward 80-plus people in the traditional paradigm will hit a growth ceiling (due to staffing capacity) when it reaches 80 to 100 people—exactly in the range of the national average church size. The church concludes they need to "add" staff to "grow." Unfortunately, their paradigm becomes, "We can't add staff *until* we grow. We can't afford it."

So today's paradigms/models ("paid staff do the heavy lifting" and "we can only do what we can financially afford") actually self-sabotage a church, paralyzing it at fewer than 100 people. The church becomes caught in the tension between the subtraction and addition culture magnets (tensions).

As it has been said, it is hard to get someone to understand something when their salary depends on them *not* understanding it.

Alan's Insight

The impact is even more pronounced in Level 3 churches that want to break free of the addition magnet's grip and move to Levels 4 and 5. The graphic below is spot on. The same strong magnet (or culture) that pulls a church into greater levels of addition-growth is the very one that keeps it from moving to greater levels of multiplication.

Levels 1, 2, 3, 4 and 5

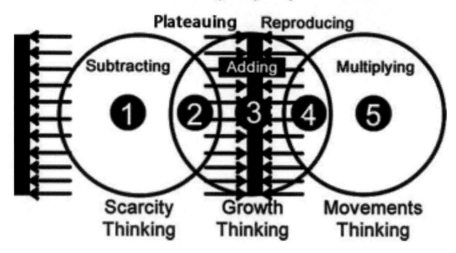

Alan's Insight

In organizational theory, this magnetic force is called a "success trap." It happens when organizations focus on the exploitation of their (historically successful) current business activities and consequently neglect the need to explore new territory and adapt. The success trap is always an issue for corporate culture. Because it was created based on the understanding of what makes for success, corporate culture solidifies around that metric. When the environment changes, a company will often initially dismiss the significance of the change and then (over time) fully experience the impact of their failure to address the change and adjust their strategy.

Specifically, the macro-addition strategies used to conquer the progressive growth barriers in Level 3 include things like large, growing specialty staff; facilities with large mortgage debt; organizational/structural complexity required to manage numerous ministries and sites; and a huge demand for volunteers and strong volunteer leaders, etc.

The financial and leadership resources required to feed the beast in Level 3 are the same resources needed to fuel multiplication in Levels 4 and 5. When this tyranny of the OR emerges, addition-growth usually wins out over multiplication. The practices and behaviors required in Levels 4 and 5 always seem to be in tension with the allocation of resources to fuel what has already been built in Level 3.

The addition magnet (culture) simply overpowers most churches that desire increasing levels of multiplication.

A key aspect of movement-thinking is to recognize that Jesus has given His church everything it needs to get the job done. The answer to all the problems we face is in the DNA that is already coded by the Spirit into the life of Jesus' people. The early church was coded for Jesus movement. We can recover this DNA if we are willing.

Alan's Insight

There is another magnet to the right of Level 5. This one is built into the intended DNA of the church by its Founder. Unfortunately, most churches are so captive to the addition culture in Level 3 that they never get close enough to the multiplication magnet to see its force field overtake the embedded addition culture.

Levels 1, 2, 3, 4 and 5

Plateauing   Reproducing

Subtracting   Adding   Multiplying

1 **2** **3** **4** **5**

Scarcity   Growth   Movements
Thinking   Thinking   Thinking

As churches venture beyond their current walls and reproduce sites (campuses), they functionally press into Level 4 practices. However, most current multisite activity is rooted in Level 3 macro-addition rather than Level 5 multiplication (multisite as a multiplication strategy has yet to be demonstrated). In terms consistent with Chapter 2, multisite is typically about building local church capacity via macro-addition rather than Kingdom capacity via new, autonomous churches (macro-multiplication).

The multisite movement is heading in the right direction, but when it's an extension of megachurch approaches to church, multisite's thinking and processes are largely rooted in the previous church growth (addition) paradigm.

Alan's Insight

However, the underlying elements of reproduction that multisite requires do position it as a possible springboard to becoming a Level 5 multiplying church. A growing number of church leaders are beginning to press into future multisite models as a strategy toward Level 5. In fact, Exponential hosts a "Radical Multisite" Learning Community for leaders who have moved beyond "how do we add more sites?" to "how do we leverage multisite for multiplication?"

Putting It Into Perspective

As a linear progression, most U.S. churches are born into Levels 1 or 2, but as we've said earlier few (we believe less than 0.05 percent) ever make it to Level 5. Overcoming the subtraction magnet (culture) and then the addition magnet (culture) is a major challenge. The normal path is linear with progression from Level 1 to 2 to 3 to 4 to 5. It's like a funnel with 80 percent at one end and virtually 0 percent making it to the other end.

Alan's Insight

The eternal punishment for the ancient mythological figure Sisyphus was to roll a boulder up a steep mountain, only to have it roll back down to the bottom each time he reached the top. In his famous essay, the French philosopher Albert Camus called Sisyphus an "absurd hero," because he struggled perpetually without any hope of success. The Greek myth easily describes the tragedy of the situation for many well-meaning church leaders today. So much of our efforts go into maintaining non-productive modes of church. We can keep doing what we've always done...or we can change. God wants His church to grow. We don't have to futilely push boulders up hill. There is a way forward.

Here are several summary truths about tensions to think about and embrace:

- Most churches are born into Level 1 or 2. The subtraction or scarcity culture is a strong shaping factor that can hold churches captive to decision making that's rooted in survival thinking. Some 80 percent of churches live at Levels 1 and 2.

- Approximately 16 percent of churches find themselves moving toward Level 3, addition-growth. The Level 3 addition magnet is extremely powerful. It fosters a culture that aligns most everything the church does to macro-addition strategies. If they're not intentional about multiplying, these churches may unintentionally replace the target of making biblical disciples with addition-growth.

- Approximately 4 percent of churches put some Level 4 practices in place. However, the Level 3 addition magnet is so strong that these churches have a difficult time breaking free from addition culture's grip, and many continue functioning with Level 3 behaviors.

- Less than 0.05 percent of U.S. churches find themselves functioning as Level 5 multiplying churches. By leaning into multiplication and putting the practices of Level 5 churches into place, we will increasingly expose ourselves to the multiplication magnet that is embedded, but suppressed, within the church's DNA.

Two possible pathways of change lead to Level 5: evolutionary change, which is linear and incremental; and revolutionary change, which throws off the shackles of the status quo to lean into and live out a new normal. Our default pathway is evolutionary and rarely produces Level 5 churches. *Is it possible we need courageous leaders willing to embrace revolutionary change and chart new pathways?*

The art of missional thinking recognizes that the church is responsible to deliver the message of Jesus in radically different and constantly changing cultural conditions. We see this task as nothing less than helping change the tracks of history.

Alan's Insight

No matter where a church currently finds itself, it can choose to put Level 5 multiplication practices in place; maybe not all at once, but one step at a time. The gap between aspirations and practice *can* be closed.

Regardless of a church's current size or level, we believe revolutionary change will start with the courageous leaders who are willing to embrace a new scorecard rooted in the values of multiplication, characterized by the practices of Level 5 churches, and squarely focused on making and mobilizing biblical disciples on mission.

Deceptions and Spiritual Warfare

As Scripture tells us, Satan is a master at deception. He came to "steal, kill and destroy" (John 10:10). His schemes are powerfully present in the dynamics that distract us from becoming the Level 5 multiplying churches we were made to be. He continually whispers lies into our minds, often seeking to feed off the unhealthy attributes of our personal scorecards. We buy into the lies and begin thinking and acting with the scarcity and growth biases of Levels 1, 2, and 3 profiles, rather than the generous and abundant behaviors of Levels 4 and 5.

Alan's Insight

Involved in this spiritual warfare are our struggles not just against personal evil (Eph.6:2) but also against key ideas and paradigms that have held us captive to being a less than fruitful expression of the Kingdom. Paul calls these the "principalities and powers" and "elemental principles," and they include an attachment to ritualistic religion, overpowering structure, as well as to unproductive concepts of the church (Gal.4:3, 8-11, Col.2:8, 13-23). Some paradigms can so dominate our thinking as to become powerful prisons for our minds and our imaginations. We need to be humble enough to let go of obsolete ideas and allow a renewed paradigm of the church to emerge. We need to dream again in Jesus about what the church really is and what it must become.

Satan is particularly good at introducing confusion that keeps us distracted. He knows that movements are fueled by Level 5 churches, so he simply needs to keep us consumed at Levels 1, 2, and 3. With 80 percent of U.S. churches at Levels 1 and 2, and fewer than 0.05 percent at Level 5, it appears he is doing his job of keeping us distracted—via two simultaneous pathways:

- First, he confuses our motives and our scorecard. Instead of embracing a more biblical scorecard of multiplication characterized by making biblical disciples, and sending/releasing leaders to multiply, we adopt the more sexy Level 3 scorecard of accumulation and consumption. We embrace the wrong scorecard.

- Second, he paralyzes us at Levels 1, 2, and 3 by making us captive to the cultures characteristic of those levels (e.g., subtraction, survival, and growth). We become so consumed and distracted within our current level that we lose sight of our intended target to make biblical disciples who make disciples. The culture we find ourselves trapped within essentially creates a different target for us to strive for—a target characterized by attaining the winning score on a particular level. It's like getting us stuck and distracted on a specific level in a video game. Our short-term target becomes "defeating the level." As we move into Level 3, we experience a culture that's nearly impossible to overcome and defeat.

Amidst these challenges, we buy into the following types of lies:

- We will [fill in the blank] when we can afford it;
- We can't [fill in the blank] until we hire another staff person, but we can't afford to hire until we grow;
- If we can just [fill in the silver bullet], we can break out of this plateau and start growing (or we can break through this next growth barrier);
- If we can get permanent facility space, then we can expand our impact;
- We will plant a church after we get stabilized and can afford it;
- Success is pioneering the latest and greatest macro-addition innovations and strategies;
- Success is breaking the next growth barrier or adding a specific number of people within a specific period of time;
- We will get our feet wet with multisite before planting a church.

The list is a mile long. In *Spark,* we highlighted 18 different tensions that churches will face in moving from Levels 1, 2, and 3 to Levels 4 and 5. However, nearly all of those tensions find their roots in three common elements: Motives, Measurements and Methods.

Three Common Core Tensions: Motives, Measurements and Methods

Below is an overview of three of the most common tensions churches face in seeking to become Level 4 and 5 multiplying churches.

Tension of Motives

The tension of motives (proximity) focuses on *here* (where we are) versus *there* (the next church). If leaders are serious about becoming a reproducing, multiplying and movement-making church, then the church they lead will start *here* but will continually need to go *there*. Not once, or twice, but continually seeking to send leaders and teams to start new churches.

Alan's Insight

As already stated, in every major choice we make, we are effectively spinning our own future. Choices matter …and they can determine so much…our future demise or our future success. The right choices made so regularly that they're now embedded into the culture of your church will eventually form a habit, and habits, in turn, shape our destiny. Make a habit of reproducing churches…starting today.

All leaders live in the tension between being *here* and *there*, with almost everything pulling them toward *here*. Having as many or more "growing there" strategies as "growing here" strategies is the difference between being a Level 3, 4, or 5 church. Movement-making churches (Level 5's) are as passionate about *there* as they are *here*.

If you're serious about being a reproducing, multiplying and movement-making church, then the church you lead will start *here*

99

but will need to go *there…there…there and there*! But understand, the tension between focusing *here* and going *there* will always exist.

Alan's Insight

The choices we make must be guided by a bigger vision of the church than the one we currently have. This is one of the aspects of the power of having a movemental vision of the church…having an idea of the church big enough to really change the world! As the 20th century Austrian poet Rilke said, "The future must enter you long before it happens."

The church planting network I (Dave) am a part of, NewThing Network, developed a tool called "My Reproducing Plan (MRP)." We ask our affiliated churches to update their MRP yearly. It's a form of accountability amidst the addition-growth tensions. In their MRP, leaders dream about and commit in writing to what they will do in the coming year. The MRP pulls planters away from only *here* thinking and toward *there* behaviors. With this tool, we aim to help churches overcome the strong bias to accumulation *here* (prevalent in Level 3), to releasing and sending *there* (Levels 4 and 5). In short, the MRP is another tool for helping you do what you say you want to do! You can download a free copy of it at exponential.org/mrp.

The tension of motives is about declaring this day that multiplication matters and embracing it as a core value—not just a nice program to add on, but also a value that shapes and influences your decisions, strategy, staffing, facilities, and budget. With any transition to a new core value comes the need for a new scorecard and lens for defining and measuring success.

Tension of Measurement

Do I grow *here* or do I send people to other places? The tension of motives (*here* versus *there*) starts with a clear mission, vision, and strategy for multiplication. But once you deal with tension of motives, you will continually face the tension of measurement:

Will we be only about growing our church, *or* will we also be about sending? Will our scorecard be biased to accumulating and consuming or releasing and sending?

 The word "sending" here is the same word as the root of the word for mission (*missio* = "sent" in Latin). And it's different from standard forms of metrics that we ordinarily use. Our commitment to "send" measures our impact beyond the church, not just in the church.

Alan's Insight

In the tension of measurement, hard questions surface:

- How much energy are we directing toward optimizing systems at the mother church vs. the amount of energy we're directing toward a system to develop leaders and staff to send to a new church plant?

- Are we hanging on to our best staff members, or sending them out as church planters?

- Are we developing our best leaders to run our programs and staff the mother church, or are we intentionally growing leaders to send them out?

- Do we have an excellent leadership residency program? Have we emphasized excellence in our leadership development/sending structures?

Level 5 churches focus on sending *as much as* growing. We will never see a level 5 movement-making church in the United States until we are as passionate about sending as we are growing. When we embrace new scorecards focused on releasing and sending leaders, we must then rethink our addition-focused behaviors and methods to realign them with multiplication.

The idea of becoming a sending church raises issues about "why" we should be a sending church in the first place. This takes us to the core theology of the church as the primary human agency of the Kingdom of God. There is therefore no such thing as an "un-sent" Christian! (John 20:21 cf. Matt. 28:19.) We send because all Christians and all churches are sent by God into the world.

Alan's Insight

At this point, the conversation moves from "dream" (what we *want* to do) to practical and personal (what we *will* do). This is where courageous leadership makes all the difference. This is where the culture-shaping decisions come to life. This is where we sweat, but also where we live out our core values with integrity.

Tension of Methods

Our methods (or practices and behaviors) are where we bring a multiplication culture to life. At the core of the tension of methods is how we allocate our time (activities), talents (leadership), and treasures (finances) to building local AND Kingdom capacity. How do we balance the tension between building local capacity to grow bigger local churches, *and* building global capacity to send and release resources to start new churches?

Three specific multiplication tensions center on actual execution and the difficult decisions leaders will need to address and resolve as they seek to build local and Kingdom capacity:

- Facilities and place
- Finances
- Relaxing versus risk-taking

Facilities and place:

In the U.S. church one of the tensions that leaders will quickly experience is the reality of needing facilities and place: Do I build buildings or plant more churches? Do I send out my first staff before I build? Do I start a new church before I build?

Make no mistake. Buildings can be a great help to accomplishing the Great Commission. People like having a "place." Most churches see an attendance bump with new spaces. *But* they can also be a hindrance to the mission because buildings are a huge expense, costing both money and time to raise the capital. They require upkeep (more money and time), and they often create an unintended culture that focuses on *here* versus *there*.

Sending out people to plant a church before the church takes on significant building debt sends a very specific message to the church and instills a multiplication DNA. The likelihood of becoming a Level 4 or 5 multiplying church significantly increases when we choose Level 4 and 5 behaviors over Level 3 behaviors.

The building issue gives us numerous questions and decisions for us to wrestle through:
- Do we put more time in our church planting strategy than we do in our future facility strategy?
- If we do decide that a building will move our mission forward, how will we use that platform to attract and train more leadership residents and church planters?

Level 4 and 5 churches also live in the tension: "Do I build a building?" or "Do I plant churches?" Their bias is toward planting as they figure out the "and."

Alan's Insight

This "facilities and place" tension highlights a theological confusion in the minds of most Christians who identify a church building with the church (ecclesia) itself. A building can house a movement but can never contain it. A movement exists outside of any buildings. It is a force in society. Buildings say "come," while the Great Commission says "go," and as a result buildings sometimes work against a church becoming a sending church. Buildings are just tools - arguably a necessary tool perhaps - but nonetheless we should never confuse them with the essence of the church as a movement.

Finances:

In Luke 14 Jesus tells His disciples that they will need to count the cost of following Him. For churches that want to ignite a culture of multiplication, very real costs and risks are involved—particularly in a financial sense. Without a strong core conviction to multiply, leaders will gravitate toward financial security instead of doing the hard work of navigating perceptions and questions. For example:

- Key givers in a church will naturally want to know the return on investment in planting new churches.
- Staff and other leaders will wonder how prioritizing the church's financial resources toward multiplication will impact their current ministries.
- Resources allocated to multiplication are not available for the local addition-growth activities that fuel attendance growth.

Alan's Insight

A church's budget says a lot about what it truly believes and values. Resource allocation can be a very useful metric for determining whether or not you really believe in multiplication. Some missional leaders insist that a genuine missional movement spends around 50 percent of the budget on mission beyond the congregation! As such, it is investing in the future of the church as movement.

Just like church leaders teach, "Look at your checkbook to know your true priorities," the same is true for a church.

- Will our church at least tithe to church planting on capital campaigns and other special offerings, as well as general offerings?
- Will our church sacrifice to plant a church?
- Will our church put funds toward training church planters and developing a leadership residency?

Relaxing versus risk-taking:

Many senior leaders find themselves in a comfortable place in Level 3. The financial strains of addition-growth are different than those in the survival culture of Levels 1 and 2. They have planted their church and have worked hard to grow it. Their church has grown to a certain size, and they're drawing a good salary. They are at a place in their leadership where they make more impact with less effort just because their words have more weight now.

The questions then become:
- After working really hard for years, do I just relax now? Or do I keep taking risks?
- What about starting a network? Or a whole movement of churches?
- Am I building systems that allow me to coast/relax, or am I still engaged and taking risks?

• Am I investing myself in the next generation of church multipliers with the same zeal I gave to conquering the Level 3 growth barriers?

Navigating this tension and these questions requires leaders to honestly assess their personal energy and resiliency.

Alan's Insight

In movements, the ability to take strategic risks is a vital element of mDNA (missional DNA). By taking regular risks for the Kingdom, church leaders develop and maintain a sense of "tribal" connection among the members of the community. A common task changes the way people relate to each other...especially if it is challenging. Think about a sports team in this light. They are comrades and not just associates. History favors the brave.

Moving Forward

In this chapter, we've highlighted the most common types of tensions you'll face in seeking to move beyond addition thinking to multiplication thinking. Be prepared. This is a dangerous journey and will require you to put to death some of the things you've grown to idolize. Overcoming these tensions takes courage, persistence and intentionality.

One of the greatest tensions we face centers around sacrifice and surrender. To conquer the Level 3, addition-growth scorecard, we must put to death the motives, measures and methods and be courageous change makers who buck the old wineskins opting for new, and better, wineskins.

Alan's Insight

When we commit to a vision of doing something that has never been done before, there is no blueprint or model. We simply have to build the bridge as we walk on it. And remember, no advancement or development would have ever been achieved if someone hadn't broken from the herd and charted a different (and better) way. Innovation is vital to the flourishing of the church.

In the process, growing through our tensions will require us to take holy risks. If you feel called to build a multiplication culture in your church, be prepared to face the "Kingdom math" gut-wrenching realities of tension.

Ours is not a question of whether or not we should grow our churches. Growth is good. The more important question is whether the increase will come through addition-growth or multiplication-growth.

Ask yourself this: *If your future and the future of your children and their children depended on you becoming a Level 5 multiplying church, what would you do differently than what you're doing now?* What would you stop doing? What would you start doing? What would you do with urgency?

In a paraphrased adaptation of Joshua's words to the Israelites: "Choose for yourselves this day ... what level of multiplication will you choose. As for me and my church, we will make biblical disciples and become a Level 5 multiplying church!"

What's stopping you?

Chapter 5
Engaging the Movement
Operating System
(Alan Hirsch)

Author and marketing guru Seth Godin schools us in the significance of perspective when he suggests that if you were able to shrink the earth to the size of a billiard ball, it would be the smoothest sphere ever created. That is, unless you were living near the edge of the Grand Canyon. Chances are then you'd find it very hard to believe.

This insight can only be gained from perspective. To put it another way, without a larger vision we can't seem to see the forest for the trees. With the right viewpoint we can discern the larger context.

So when we look at the metaphor of *movement*, realize the importance of viewpoint here. Movement thinking provides us with the overall perspective that allows us to assess where we currently are and what we're currently doing. The metaphor of *movement* gets us close to the paradigm that will unlock the power of Jesus' people. Movement was at the heart of the New Testament vision of the church, and I (Alan) am excited that it's once again beginning to work its way into the language and imaginations of tens of thousands of leaders across the Western world.

In the previous chapters, we've focused on the *why* and *what* of multiplication—both irreplaceable aspects of every transformative gospel movement. Now we need to put the multiplication challenge of becoming five into its broader context and take a close look at what it means to become a full-fledged Level 5 *movement*. In this chapter, we're introducing you to the necessary dimensions of movement thinking that can help us see what God is doing and hopefully join Him in that mission.

For more vital detail on movement thinking, we strongly encourage you to study books from Dave Ferguson (*Exponential*,

On The Verge), Alan Hirsch (*The Forgotten Ways*, *The Permanent Revolution* and *Fast Forward to Mission*), Neil Cole (*Church 3.0*), Ed Stetzer (*Viral Churches*) and Steve Addison (*Movements That Change the World*) among others.

Questions and the Quest

As you've no doubt experienced while reading this book, the move toward becoming a Level 5 church causes us to ask probing questions about our current understanding and practices of church—difficult questions that begin to tell us what we truly value. Church growth or broader Kingdom impact?

1. What do I really think about growth and multiplication?
2. Does that thinking help or hinder our leadership and church from seeing the issues clearly?
3. What are the roles of structure and organization in our church? How do these roles impact movement thinking?
4. Does the culture of our church enhance or prevent movement?
5. Are we willing to make the necessary changes and trust ourselves to the triumph of Jesus in and through His people by investing in the future of the church as multiplication movement?

Most importantly, in *Becoming Five* we've attempted to highlight the need to shift our current system from addition to reproducing, and then from reproducing to multiplication. If we want to see churches planted, then we must intentionally set out to plant churches. But if we want to see genuine multiplication, then we have to plant reproducing churches.

In a sense, we've thrown down the gauntlet to the overwhelming majority of churches across North America that have settled for subtraction and addition to take the challenge and make the necessary choices that we (Alan, Dave and Todd) believe could alter the flow of history.

A Movement Mindset

To answer the call to multiply, we first have to win the battle for the imagination. Our primary paradigms, rationales and frameworks must change. In many ways, the paradigm is the "brain of the organization" and provides the reasoning for our actions and practices. Bottom line, to become a movement we have to first—and foremost—learn to *think* like a movement.

We need a movement mindset.

Perhaps another powerful contemporary metaphor might drive this point home: Like the operating system (the OS) in your computer or smart phone, the primary paradigm provides the *platform* for the launch of hundreds of thousands of possible applications (programs). The OS determines if you can run certain desired apps or programs.

If you want to become a Level 5 multiplying church, then you'll need the right operating system; the wrong system will never produce Level 5 results. Fundamentally however, it is first and foremost a matter of imagination.

Consider the following diagram that guides the process we're using for 100 Movements, an organization I'm involved in that's seeking to identify and train 100 movement-minded churches and ministries across North America to become competent as Level 5 movements.

The *first image* reflects the dominant imagination of the church—the standard Christendom understanding of the church. The overwhelming majority of churches in the West think of church this way. Basically, this mindset derives from the European understanding of the church. It's an unhappy face because I believe there is a realization that what has brought us to this point in history is simply not going to get us to where we want to be in a viable future. The fact that you're even reading this book and have gotten this far supports that. Many of our current problems come because we're using a "traditional" operating system (paradigm)— an OS from an entirely different era with a distinctly different, *non-movemental* mindset.

The battle for the church in the future will first and foremost happen as a battle for the imagination (*second image*). Once we have grasped the paradigm of movement, then the challenge is to go from paradigm to practice (*third image*) and ultimately to generate authentic movement (*fourth image*).

Putting Movement Into Practice

When we activate the more fundamental movement operating system latent in every church—represented by the "movement swoosh" in the diagram—the church will get much closer to the initial movemental paradigm we find in the New Testament church. Not only does this just feel right at the deepest level, we also wind up with the right vision and imagination to develop movemental thinking and practices in the whole life of the church. This way, we get movement out of our dreams and into the church. If our non-movemental OS doesn't change, we will have little hope of seeing a movement of multiplying churches and biblical disciples. Essentially, we must move from paradigm to practice.

I (Alan) realize and fully admit this is more difficult than it sounds. As we've already observed, we're addicted to past paradigms of the church, and we have plenty of organizational habits that confine our church to its current level of multiplication, whether it's Level 1, 2 or 3. Habits, especially religious ones, can be extremely difficult to change. Here comes the vital work of translating movement *thinking* into movement *practice*.

Once we as leaders "get" the paradigm into our own hearts and heads, it's quite another to get it from there and into the church! Be warned. When you experience the necessary paradigm shift to Level 5 thinking, you'll quickly discover that so many of our deeply embedded practices of church bind us in the inherently non-movemental paradigms of Level 1 to Level 3.

Churches willing to pursue Level 5 will require:
• real courage;
• a theologically structured vision;
• a whole lot of leadership can-do;
• a resolute determination to get to Level 5 regardless of their starting point.
A comprehensive list. *But it can be done.* By resolving to "recode" your church's OS around movement, you'll work towards what God originally designed and intended—and you'll have divine support. *He* will build the movement, and the gates of Hell will not prevail against it.

Level 5 *Multiplication* Requires a Level 5 *System*

In the previous chapters, we've focused on inspiring leaders and churches to see the power of multiplication thinking and make choices to move in that direction. By now, you've probably taken the tests at the beginning of the book and have a viable assessment of your current situation, as well as what level you want to aspire to (if at all). Our hope is that by shifting the metrics from addition to reproducing to multiplication, we can give leaders a viable pathway for a movement to emerge from their current expressions of church.

So while movements will never happen without a deep commitment to multiplication and a determination to align the organization around reproducing, other key aspects of movement will require attention, as well as a scalable process. Yes, real multiplication is absolutely necessary for movements to take place, but *by itself* multiplication is not sufficient to generate or maintain sustainable, long-term impact. The one key element for a genuine movement is the right operating system. Granted, it's not a silver bullet, but it is a crucial part of a silver imagination.

The good news is that while multiplication is not sufficient by itself, it is more than enough to trigger and activate the factors already latent within the Church's DNA. Know that if you set out to become a Level 5 multiplying church, you'll need to keep your eyes on other key elements that are vital to creating a full-fledged movement OS—generating a movement that can truly change the world.

This movemental thinking and practice has been the cornerstone of my (Alan's) life work, and I'm convinced more than ever before that it is fundamentally correct, so much so that everything I do (including my writing, speaking and work with 100 Movements, Forge and Exponential) is tied into this. I'm a committed believer. As far as I can discern, whenever all six elements I've identified (called mDNA in *The Forgotten Ways*) come into play, then a high impact Jesus movement is already happening.

Briefly, these six elements include:

1) Identifying ourselves in relation to the defining reality of Jesus as Lord;
2) Prioritizing discipleship and disciple making;
3) Practicing incarnational (adaptive) forms of mission;
4) Cultivating the kind of communities that thrive in risk and adventure;
5) Developing scalable organizations that can spread across a wide distance;
6) Generating a missional leadership culture.

For a more comprehensive description of the deep change process required to activate movements, check out the book I wrote with Dave Ferguson called *On The Verge*. Also, the training organization I work with, 100 Movements, is built entirely around a long-term process of helping churches and organizations multiply.

For the purposes of this book, we can represent the movement system, what I call Apostolic Genius, in the diagram below:

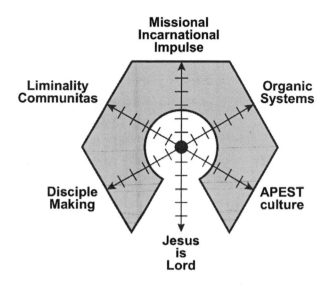

I can only give a basic outline of each of the elements here, enough for you to discern the importance of each of these in developing a movement OS. In the headings below, the mDNA is stated and the associated competency is in brackets. Consider the following as teasers…

Jesus is Lord (competency: declaring who and whose we are!)

At the center and circumference of every significant Jesus movement, there exists a very simple but profound confession. The confession of "Jesus is Lord" vibrates with the primal energies of the scriptural faith. Putting Jesus—His life and teaching—front and center in the church gives as a very clear, distinctly Jesus-shaped understanding of who God is.

To be authentic, the life of the disciple and the church must correspond to the life of Jesus. But in the claim of His lordship, Jesus also claims the right to rule over every aspect of our lives, *and* He has the right to rule over the response of His people to His claim of Lordship (Deut. 6:4–6ff.). By living into this simple confession, movements change the world.

Truth is, the body of Christ can never take for granted the exemplary role of Jesus. Any commitment to multiplication forces us to ask hard, telling questions:

- Do we know who we are in relation to Jesus?
- What exactly are we seeking to multiply?
- Do we know what our core message is?
- Are we living consistently with that radical message?
- Do we conform to the revolutionary life, teachings and commands of our founder and Lord Jesus Christ?

Make no mistake, very bad religion can be very effectively spread simply by using very good multiplication methodology—(if you need convincing, look no further than the Jihadist religion of Al Qaeda and ISIS). As horrifying as it might seem to us as insiders, we must ask ourselves: Are we extending a toxic religion? All of us need a regular visit with Jesus to see if we're being true to His cause!

Our method must be consistent with our message. This recalibrating of the church around Jesus—what I call *reJesus*—requires penetrating self-analysis and honest, collective discernment. In 100 Movements, we call the competency related to Jesus is Lord, "identity declaring," because it means that we have to declare who we are in relation to Jesus.

Jesus is Lord! This is the message we're called to reproduce and deliver to a lost world.

Discipleship (competency: disciple making)

Essentially, discipleship involves the irreplaceable and lifelong task of becoming like Jesus by embodying His message. It also involves Jesus living his life through us. Perhaps this idea can be

116

captured by defining discipleship *as doing the kind of things that Jesus did for the same reasons that He did them.* Perhaps this is where many of our efforts fail. Disciple making is a core purpose of the church and needs to be structured into every church's basic ministry.

At this point in time, the Western church is pretty good at making cultural Christians, but not so hot at making genuine disciples. Discipleship is necessary; it is how the church actually becomes like Christ in all aspects of life. It's how Jesus' presence is made manifest in the life of the individual and the church. A Level 5 OS requires:

• a very clear definition of discipleship;
• a strategic commitment to make it unavoidable in the life of the average Christian;
• clear pathways for personal discipleship leading to multiplication disciple making.

Missional-Incarnational Impulse (competency: incarnational messaging).

This third mDNA element suggests that there are two related dimensions in the mission of outstanding multiplication missional movements. These are the dynamic *outward* impulses (going out in mission) and the related *deepening* one (going deep through incarnation). This has to do with how movements extend themselves into new and often uncharted territory. Together, these impulses seed and embed the gospel into different cultures and people groups.

While *mission* takes the church's "sentness" seriously and assumes responsibility to spread the gospel, *incarnational mission*— following as it does in the Way of the Incarnate One—will always engage culture from the inside out. This means, among other things, meaningfully translating the Good News of Jesus and grounding it in the life of a given people and/or in a particular place—what 100 Movements calls the competency of *incarnational messaging*.

Because 100M is committed to planting the gospel in new soil and subsequently seeing new forms of church emerge, incarnational mission really is the mother of all ecclesial innovation. To commit to incarnational messaging requires that we learn how to innovate in many different contexts. Generally preferring the cookie-cutter, plug-and-play church models, most churches passionately resist any form of innovation. We have some learning (and unlearning) to do if we're going to have an impact for the gospel in our increasingly complex, multicultural, tribalized world.

Liminality-Communitas (competency: risk-tribalizing)

The most vigorous forms of community are those that come together in the context of a shared ordeal, or those that define themselves as a group with a mission beyond and bigger than themselves—thus initiating a risky journey. Too much concern with safety and security, combined with comfort and convenience, has lulled us out of our true calling and purpose.

We all love an adventure. Or do we?

History favors the brave, and in times of significant crisis, those who are willing to confront the challenges of the day will pave the way for many others to follow. The trick is to maintain and deepen the sense of tribal identity as we take risks. Risk-taking, in turn, generates deep bonds of fellowship. Movements are very good at this. At the heart of the community-tribe, we fund a deep sense of bonding and comradeship.

If we are to become a genuine multiplication movement, we will need to become far more adventurous than we tend to be now. Jesus seeks to transform the world through the Church, and it will take more than Sunday attendance and a weekly prayer group if we're going to be equal to the task.

For further exploration, check out *The Faith of Leap: A Theology of Adventure and Risk* by Alan Hirsch and Michael Frost (Grand Rapids: Baker, 2012).

APEST culture (competency: leader releasing).

This fifth element of the mDNA describes the necessity of all the ministry and leadership styles referenced in Ephesians 4:1-16 and demonstrated by the church in the book of Acts, namely the apostolic, prophetic, evangelistic, shepherding, and teaching (APEST) functions. This mDNA relates to the type of ministry and leadership required to sustain exponential growth and transformational impact.

Engaging APEST involves widening our understanding to include the more movemental ministry led by all five leadership capacities. Our inherited understandings of ministry derived from Europe have disastrously limited leadership to that of the shepherd (pastor) and teacher (theologian). And while these functions are absolutely necessary to sustain movement over the long term, they generally lack the entrepreneurial agility to generate, catalyze and design movemental forms of church. History is absolutely clear on this. The other three ministry functions—apostolic (missional), prophetic and evangelistic—are definitely more generative in nature and purpose. We and numerous other leaders are completely convinced that APEST culture is a critical missing link in our operating system.

For a deep exploration of this critical mDNA, read *The Permanent Revolution: Apostolic Imagination and Practice for the 21st Century Church* (San Francisco: Jossey Bass, 2012) by Tim Catchim and Alan Hirsch; and the associated group study *The Permanent Revolution Playbook* (Denver: Missio, 2015).

Organic Systems: (competency: multiplication organizing)

Because we've already majored on this element of movement thinking, I (Alan) don't need to say much more on this sixth mDNA element except to highlight how putting it into the context of the other elements of DNA shows how they are all profoundly interconnected.

Becoming a multiplication movement requires us to initiate certain practices. You'll need to engage more movemental forms of leadership; prioritize disciple making; innovate new forms of church on mission; and create a culture of risk-taking and comradeship, etc.

So once again, an authentic multiplication movement includes:

1. A radical and unwavering commitment to the ethos of the founder, Jesus, which must inform everything we do;
2. A clearly articulated vision for discipleship as well as a clear process to ensure that disciple making happens throughout the organization;
3. A commitment to extend the movement by going out and going deep into various cultures and interpreting the gospel into these settings;
4. A missional ministry (and by extension, leadership) equal to the task of initiating, developing, and maintaining movement;
5. A system designed around internalized mDNA, committed to empowering every agent in the system by pushing power and function to the outermost limits, along with a resolute pre-commitment to system-wide reproducibility and scalability;
6. An inbuilt, culturally embedded willingness to regularly dare and to take risks in the cause of the movement.

When all of these elements come together … movement becomes a reality, and we won't just be dreaming about or imagining a movement of multiplication. We will be one.

We shall not cease from exploration
And the end of all our exploring
Will be to arrive where we started
And know the place for the first time.[6]
~ T.S. Eliot "Little Gidding"

Appendix: Profiles of Multiplying Churches

Levels 1, 2, 3, 4 and 5

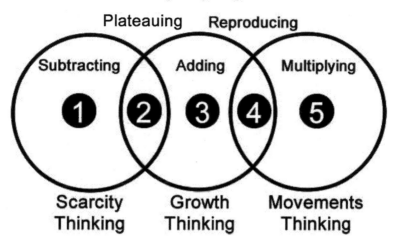

Profiles: Five Levels of Multiplying Churches

Level 1 Profile:

The primary characterizations of Level I churches are "subtraction, scarcity, and survival." Typically, Level 1 churches live with financial tension because they are always worried about having enough money to keep the lights on for Sunday services. They struggle to pay a full-time pastor and then strive toward being able to afford their own facility. As they move to Level 2, most Level 1 churches secure permanent facilities, only exacerbating their financial instability. The continuing financial tensions produce a scarcity mindset that shapes their culture and how they approach ministry.

While the majority of Level 1 churches are small (the average size church in the U.S. runs under 100 attendees), larger churches that have experienced an attendance decline can also be Level 1. The decline produces a financial tension similar to what a smaller church experiences. In a smaller church, the tension is having enough money to pay a full-time pastor and get a building; in a larger church it's having enough money to pay the current staff and a mortgage that may have been secured when more people were giving to the church.

In either case, Level 1 churches operate out of a scarcity mindset. Their planning doesn't look too much beyond getting done what needs to be done for the next couple of weeks. Multiplication doesn't come to mind, and church planting isn't even on the radar. Below are some of the common characteristics of a Level 1 church that you can use to determine where your church is currently:

The senior pastor is running hard to keep up with everything in front of him or her. He is the one that must make all the decisions and hospital visits, officiate weddings and funerals, do the sermon prep, etc. The exhaustive to-do list doesn't leave much time for developing leaders, and he hopes that people are being discipled by his messages. Due to the breadth of the senior minister's responsibilities, the elders are strongly involved in the church's operations. Still, the senior pastor is the one people look to in times of crisis. In fact, in many cases he is the spiritual shepherd, teacher and hero.

The church is dependent on the weekend gatherings for financial viability. So it's not surprising that the weekend services become the focal point for the church. They are designed to satisfy the people that have been attending so the service has a familiar family feel—you usually know who will be there and where they'll be sitting.

In Level 1 churches, most spiritual conversions happen somewhere directly in the presence of the senior pastor or under his or her influence. Because the weekend services (including Sunday school and possibly a prayer service) are the church's primary expression, it isn't difficult to see why people associate "church" with a place or a building.

Churches in this profile typically don't have a systematic plan for developing leaders. While there's talk of growth, most of the energy is spent on keeping up with the needs of people and running Sunday services. Consequently, there's a tendency to lead with "No," and there's not much room for innovation.

Most Level 1 churches would be characterized as consumers rather than producers. Their lack of generosity in releasing people and resources on mission is not due to their lack of compassion and heart. Instead, it's the practical ramification of continually living within a scarcity culture. Leaders live in fear of the future rather than energized by its opportunity.

Most new U.S. church plants are born into Level 1. If they're fortunate to raise enough funds, they may temporarily find themselves in Level 2, but with a countdown clock running as they experience negative cash flow. Most church planters want to be full time with a salary, but that puts significant burden on the new church's finances. Like a business startup, a relatively short window of opportunity exists to either become financially self-sufficient and move into Levels 2 and 3; risk shutting down; or become trapped in a scarcity culture.

Most strategic and vision conversations about the future end with, "we will [fill in the blank] someday when we can afford it." Unfortunately, that elusive day rarely comes for most of the 80 percent of churches in Levels 1 and 2.

The following are a list of characteristics of Level 1 churches. This list is not exhaustive or all-inclusive, and not all Level 1 churches will exhibit all of these characteristics. Don't become overly focused on individual words or characteristics, but instead look at the totality of the culture that the list represents.

- Experiencing decline in some combination of attendance, financial giving, groups/teams, and capacity for maintaining current operations and activities;
- Lack vision and strategy for a future beyond the reality of surviving;
- Scarcity and survival penetrate, inform and shape the culture and decision making;
- Very little conversion growth with most additions through transfers;
- Sense of fear, helplessness and being trapped;
- Often focused on cutting and limiting versus investing and expanding;
- Constrained with bias to "no" rather than "yes";
- Isolated in the community with minimal collaboration in the broader mosaic of organizations impacting their community. Minimal impact or relevance to the community beyond the impact geared to its own members (not externally focused);
- Guarded, protecting and holding on;
- Centralized versus decentralized structure and decision making;
- Most "exercised" leadership is via the senior minister and elders;
- Bias to losing versus attracting staff;
- Small or limited staff and little evidence of the priesthood of all believers being mobilized on mission;
- Shepherding and teaching leadership bias over apostolic and evangelistic impulse;
- Circumstance- versus opportunity-driven;
- Resistant or reluctant to change ("We've never done it that way...");
- Crisis-focused with minimal celebration;
- Tension versus joy and energy;
- Lacking evangelistic zeal;
- Declining budgets and living with the reality of negative cash flow. ("Where should we cut?")
- Loyal core of people carrying out a disproportionate amount of the work;

124

- Weekend-centric;
- Managing versus leading;
- Unclear, confused, or out-of-alignment vision, mission, values and strategy;
- Bias to the possible versus the impossible;
- Focused on and desiring to stabilize;
- Aging (not necessarily old, but aging congregation with loss or lack of younger people and families);
- Consumed with cutting expenses and how best to add attendance numbers;
- Frequent talk about finances, including the shortfalls

Level 2 Profile:

Level 2 churches have survived and may be growing. They have growth in their sights with Level 3 at the pinnacle, but are constrained by their scarcity thinking. Their focus and aspirations center on growth and addition, and their primary characterizations are "tension, scarcity, survival, and growth."

How do we get to 100? 200? 500? What is our strategy? Do we build? Do we hire a family minister? They are consumed in identifying the actions that will move them toward Level 3. Level 2 churches are often torn by the tyranny of the *or*: "Now that we're financially stable and holding our own, do we put money into staff *or* a permanent facility?" Lacking vision and values for multiplication, the priority of actually releasing resources to multiply just doesn't measure up to the perceived reward at the top of Level 3.

Churches in this profile may be experiencing the "silver bullet syndrome" that causes them to look for that one program or activity or project that will propel them into addition growth.

The lure and appeal of graduating to Level 3 addition is very strong and consumes their thinking.

The following are a list of characteristics of Level 2 churches. This list is not exhaustive or all-inclusive, and not all Level 2 churches will exhibit all of these characteristics. Don't become overly focused on individual words or characteristics, but instead look at the totality of the culture that the list represents:

- Plateaued or possibly stuck. Their scorecard is trending sideways with static attendance, financial giving, etc.;
- Cross-current of tension between survival and growth. Their eyes are fixed on growth (Level 3), but the influence of scarcity thinking at Level 1 constantly pulls on them;
- Experiencing a mixture of characteristics from both Level 1 and Level 3, often being pulled in different directions;
- Living in the tension of, "we will [fill in blank], when we can afford it";
- More susceptible to the "silver bullet" syndrome (i.e., "if we [fill in the blank], we might catalyze growth"). They are continually looking for that important thing that will change their trajectory and put them on the path toward Level 3: Should we add a staff member, a ministry? Do a marketing campaign or outreach event? Or possibly build?
- A stability that allows the church to exhale and catch its breath while trying to figure out the best path forward to Level 3;
- Cautious, reserved, and deliberate. Small steps of risk;
- Tyranny of the OR (we can do this *or* that but not both);
- Overcoming inertia to create momentum;
- Budget-constrained (but at least not having to cut like Level 1).
- Afraid/fearful of losing people.
- Susceptible to making decisions to preserve, please and keep people happy rather than being bold to seize new opportunities;
- No (or minimal) leadership development pipeline;
- Multiplication/church planting is a distant future hope versus a current reality as it competes with limited resources within their OR mentality;
- Emerging hope and optimism (if they're moving forward from Level 1) OR increasing fear and uncertainty (if they're declining backward from Level 3). Tension, uncertainty and

fog about the future. These churches are looking for a clear picture toward Level 3;

- Leveraging gifting of staff and elders versus releasing the capacity of the church;
- Lacking clarity or strong conviction to act in alignment with vision, mission, values and strategy;
- Focusing on strategies for adding numbers consumes more time than focusing on biblical disciple making. Instinctively, the pathway to Level 3 is implementing strategies that add attendance;
- May be in the process of refining their governance and core processes to move from centralized to more decentralized approaches, with a number of simultaneous, subtle transitions happening;
- Often focused on "how do we [fill in the blank]?"
- Fearful of instability or decline;
- Church-centric. It's difficult to look beyond managing inside the church;
- Vision and strategy are unifying, but often with focus on the macro-addition strategies of Level 3

Level 3 Profile:

Level 3 churches have shown success at growth. Their leaders are conquerors with a demonstrated record of taking the next hill. The primary characterizations of these churches are "addition, growth and accumulation."

These churches have grown accustomed to finding and solving the problems that limit growth. They've dealt with rapid year-over-year growth in budgets; building and facility decisions; capital campaigns and assuming debt; building teams; staffing (including hiring and firing); structural issues (including infrastructure and overhead); the drive for the next innovative marketing and outreach strategies; and reorganizations to improve organizational alignment.

Level 3 churches live and breathe macro-addition. They are opportunity-oriented with a bias to "where or what is the next one?" They and their peers have inherited the addition-growth scorecard of their spiritual fathers and are products of the church growth movement of the past 30 years.

Churches in this profile don't *want* to fundamentally be about the numbers, but they also know that numbers matter. Income is directly proportional to attendance, and the number of volunteers needed increases as attendance numbers increase.

These churches experience a constant tension and delicate symbiotic balance between increasing attendance numbers; increasing financial giving numbers; and increasing volunteer hours. Out of necessity, staff often function as managers and coordinators rather than disciple makers. Thus, the constant tension between making biblical disciples and cultural Christians is always lurking. The time, energy, and effort needed to model biblical disciple making from the top down and the bottom up simply doesn't fit the demands of a rapid numerical growth culture. As a result, the focus shifts to "leadership development systems" rather than biblical disciple making. In case you're wondering, here's the difference between the two. *Leadership development* is more systematic and impersonal, focusing on developing skills and competencies, whereas *biblical disciple making* takes time and effort at the relational level and focuses on character, surrender, calling, and obedience.

These leadership development systems are essential to building capacity at the local level (our definition of macro-addition activities). In most cases, these systems center on the goal of supporting internal growth in the local church versus creating a source of leaders to *go*.

For these Level 3 churches, releasing resources to macro-multiplication directly competes with the very resources that fuel their macro-addition strategies. And only one wins out!

Leaders of Level 3 churches are at a crucial point in their development in terms of setting the course of their future: addition-growth culture versus multiplication-growth culture. Their choices are numerous "line in the sand" decisions that could potentially shape their core values, convictions and practices. The path for most of the churches in this profile keeps them captive and stuck, unable to move beyond Level 3 multiplication.

The following is a list of characteristics of Level 3 churches. This list is not exhaustive or all-inclusive, and not all Level 3 churches will exhibit all of these characteristics. Don't become overly focused on individual words or characteristics, but instead look at the totality of the culture that the list represents:

- Dollar-dependent versus disciple-dependent;
- Resource allocation (e.g., staff, facilities, programs) is often in support of increased "butts in seats" (attendance);
- Local capacity building is far more focused on producing and maintaining addition-growth than on making, developing and deploying biblical disciples;
- Accumulation and numerical growth;
- "Customer orientation": who is the customer, what do they value and how do we deliver that value?
- Can unintentionally mistake or overvalue participation over transformation;
- "Growth strategies" and growth seasons are never ending. Staff is often challenged with "What will we do to grow in this upcoming opportunity season?";
- Opportunity-biased ... for numerical growth;
- Adding local capacity to grow numbers. Most resources (financial and people) are put into local church growth with minimal allocated to Kingdom capacity via new churches;
- Focused on growing the church versus changing the community or city;
- Constant tension between adding cultural Christians who need to be fed AND making biblical disciples who mature to be sent;
- Leading *and* managing;

129

- These churches are learning to leverage the "genius of the AND" for growth, but not so much for multiplication;
- Allocating resources: staff, buildings, programs, outreach, marketing, etc.;
- Decentralized structure and control with increased emphasis on groups and teams;
- "Multi" thinking: multisite, multicultural, multi-service style, etc. Focused on increasing the "flavors" and "options" rather than preserving the past;
- Innovative risk-taking when it comes to addition-growth strategies;
- Debt;
- Program- and event-driven with major emphasis on Sunday services;
- Conquerors. Overcoming next barriers, obstacles and hills. Continually progressing through the next series of "false" summits to find the next one waiting;
- Staff led;
- Early adopters (and often pioneers) in the diffusion of innovation theory;
- Competitive and driven with an eye toward being on the various largest and fastest-growing churches lists;
- Opportunistic (seeing the opportunity and seizing it), especially for increased growth. Learning to discern between great and good opportunities;
- Evangelistic impulse via large group preaching and events is often stronger than the relational work of biblical disciple making (producing disciples who make disciples). Strategies at Level 3 are often characterized by churches making disciples rather than disciples making disciples;
- Often higher concentration of apostolic and evangelistic leadership;
- Excitement, energy and momentum;
- Frequent celebration, story and inspiration;
- "We can do it, you can help" versus "You can do it, we can help" approach;

- Significant resources required to "feed the beast" and run the church compared with resources allocated to developing and sending people to start new churches;
- Often values excellence;
- Scorecard: Attendance ("butts in seats"), financial giving and decisions (baptisms). Spiritual formation is often not given the same weight;
- Increasing complexity is difficult to reproduce;
- Holy discontent of senior leader may emerge ("There must be something more than simply growing things bigger.");
- The things birthed outside the walls of the church are typically connected to growth inside the church;
- Churchwide campaigns of various shapes and sizes;
- Family-friendly (e.g., often a strong children's and youth focus);
- Solid leadership development systems emerge, but often to fuel the increased required local capacity needed in the local church (rather than for sending leaders to start new churches)

Level 4 Profile:

The primary characterizations for Level 4 churches include "discontent, new scorecards, and reproducing at all levels." Leaders of these churches sense that there is something more than conquering addition-growth and are drawn to a future that's more about planting new orchards than putting more trees in their orchard.

Level 4 leaders also sense something new and fresh. Maybe they've already embraced a different scorecard, or maybe they're simply feeling a holy discontent that something needs to change. They almost instinctively know that "more of the same will not get us to where we need to go." They desire and are willing to move to Level 5, and might be making progress, but the tensions and force pulling them back to Level 3 limits their ability to move more fully into Level 5.

Level 4 churches demonstrate the ability to reproduce leaders,

131

services, and sites/campuses. But their discontent pulls them toward different motives for reproducing. Their reasons for reproduction become more about macro-multiplication to build Kingdom capacity than macro-addition to build local church capacity.

These churches are as passionate about leadership development systems that intentionally produce leaders to *go* as they are about systems that develop leaders to stay. They are birthing and taking ownership of a strong value of multiplication, including putting behaviors and practices in place that are consistent with Level 5 churches.

Level 4 churches live in tension. They are torn between a vision for multiplication at Level 5 and the reality of the demands created by Level 3 macro-addition practices. The resources needed to deploy and send for multiplication are typically the best resources for fueling Level 3 growth.

The following is a list of characteristics of Level 4 churches. This list is not exhaustive or all-inclusive, and not all Level 4 churches will exhibit all of these characteristics. Don't become overly focused on individual words or characteristics, but instead look at the totality of the culture that the list represents:

- Experiencing strong tension between the demands of macro-addition and the desire for macro-multiplication. These churches want more multiplication but feel constrained by the demands of maintaining the overhead required for the macro-addition strategies they have in place;
- Experiencing reproduction at various levels including multisite and church planting;
- Decision-making and resource allocation are still strongly influenced by Level 3 macro-addition, but these churches also have a demonstrated commitment to multiplication. They allocate resources to specific multiplication practices such as leadership internships/residencies, support services for church planters, participation in and affiliation with church planting

132

networks or associations, and direct funding of church planting;

- Reproducing happens through discipline, intentionality, and a multiplication strategy;
- These churches are often more aggressive with their multisite strategy than their church planting strategy;
- Sacrificial and generous, contributing their first fruits of leaders and money to church multiplication;
- Scorecard that includes macro-multiplication activities such as number of churches planted, number of church planters trained, percent of income allocated to church planting, and number of leaders deployed;
- These churches are as passionate about releasing and sending as they are about accumulating and growing;
- Value is placed on leadership development that leads to reproducing and multiplying churches;
- Multiplication may still be more activity-based than values-based, and may not transcend beyond the tenure of the senior pastor;
- Multiplication is typically more deliberate and planned than it is spontaneous, and often occurs with staff and interns. These churches are starting to see lay people being called and mobilized to "go" and be part of church planting;
- These churches regularly celebrate and highlight the impact of the churches they start, using the opportunity to inspire others to be involved;
- People in the church see church planting as a Kingdom-focused activity of the church that requires sacrifice;
- Leadership development pipeline is healthy and active, fueling the Level 3 activities of the church as well as church multiplication.
- Micro-multiplication is a key element of adding disciples. Biblical disciple making is strong, with disciples making disciples who make disciples. The natural fruit of this strong disciple-making culture is a pool of leaders willing to *go* and be part of starting new churches;

- People in the church are regularly called to join and be part of church planting teams, including the sacrifice to move;
- Because of their reputation, Level 4 churches tend to attract leaders from outside the church who are interested in church planting;
- Tend to start local church planting networks or affiliate with existing ones;
- Often have a full- or part-time staff person overseeing their church planting activities;
- Senior leaders have a natural "holy discontent" that causes a bias for action toward Level 5 behaviors;
- Exhibit significant financial commitment to church planting;
- Releasing staff is more intentional in Level 4 compared with Level 3 where it is often reactive;
- Collaborative, teachable bias with Kingdom perspective;
- Heart for the lost;
- Competition is no longer other churches, but instead the obstacles to increased multiplication;
- *Go* culture and bias

Level 5 Profile:

Level 5 churches are rare, so they stick out in the crowd. The primary characterizations for these churches are "multiplying, releasing, and sending." Their leaders spend as much time on macro-multiplication strategies and activities as they do on macro-addition.

Churches in this profile will plant hundreds of churches and send thousands of people to be part of church planting teams over their lifespan. Their scorecard is more about "who has been sent" than "how many have been accumulated." They demonstrate many of the same characteristics of Level 3 and 4 churches, but are distinguished by behaviors:

- Level 5 churches have church planting interns/residents in training who will be sent to launch new churches within the next 12 months.

- They are more focused on multiplying new churches than they are on growing their own church larger and conquering the next attendance barrier.

- They contribute substantial financial resources (at least 10 percent) from the first fruits of their budget to church planting. They are continually looking for ways to increase and leverage the amount. They also tithe (at least) to church planting on any funds raised for buildings and mortgage debt.

- They choose to plant their first autonomous church before assuming land and building debt.

- They decide to plant their first autonomous church before launching their own first campus or multisite.

- They have a specific plan for doubling their church planting activity—not a dream or vision, but rather a specific plan for guiding and making it happen.

- They release and send out their first church planter before accumulating several staff members, and then they continue to send staff, releasing the first fruits of their leadership capacity in a regular and ongoing way.

- They publicly and regularly call their members to *go* and be part of church planting teams.

- They regularly celebrate their church planting activities in a way that inspires others to get involved. They celebrate in a way that helps people see how they can be involved versus simply hearing about what others are doing.

- They publicly and regularly call their members to give sacrificially above and beyond their tithe to the local church to support church planting and specific church plants.

- They are actively affiliated with and participating in a church planting network (or denominational initiative) that's committed to multiplication. Often, they are the founding members of these networks.

Churches that consistently practice and exhibit these behaviors close the gap between aspirations and reality. The persistent focus and sacrifice toward macro-multiplication creates a culture of multiplication in these churches. These Level 5 churches develop a DNA so strongly centered on multiplication that they would have to *try* not to multiply.

The following is a list of characteristics of Level 5 churches. This list is not exhaustive or all-inclusive, and not all Level 5 churches will exhibit all of these characteristics. Don't become overly focused on individual words or characteristics, but instead look at that totality of the culture that the list represents:

- These churches would have to *try* not to multiply. Multiplication is deeply embedded in their DNA;
- Multiplication seems to happen spontaneously and is not limited to paid staff;
- Mobilize the priesthood of all believers;
- Biblical disciple making is strong, with much of the church's growth occurring as disciples make disciples who make disciples;
- Strategies are simple and reproducible;
- Have a different scorecard rooted in sending and releasing capacity versus adding and accumulating;
- Solid balance of the Ephesians five-fold gifting and with a strong apostolic impulse;
- Aggressive intern and residency program (leadership development pipeline leading to church plants);
- Focused on pastoring and transforming a city/geographic area versus building and growing a church;

136

- Significant commitment of financial resources to macro-multiplication (e.g., >10+ of tithes and offerings);
- Routinely releasing staff AND members to planting;
- Every disciple is a potential church planter/team member;
- Daughter church plants carry the DNA and are also active in church planting/sending;
- Decision making and resource allocation is always through the lens of church multiplication;
- Activities and commitment transcend the tenure of the senior pastor;
- Marketplace/lay leaders are routinely released/sent to plant churches;
- Regular and ongoing celebration of multiplication stories and impact;
- Regularly call members to sacrifice financially in giving to church planting. These churches are as inclined to run church-planting campaigns as they are church-building campaigns;
- Have systems to develop, deploy and support church-planting leaders and teams;
- Regularly coach and help leaders outside the church who are planting churches;
- Often part of (or founding members in) a church planting network or association;
- Develop best practices for others to follow;
- Solid balance between macro-addition and macro-multiplication;
- Abundance mentality with a big vision and goals for impact beyond the walls of the church;
- "Spiritual fathers" to children, grandchildren, and great grandchild churches;
- Movement mentality

Other Free Resources on Multiplication

All of the following are available for FREE download from Exponential. Visit https://www.exponential.org/resource-ebooks/ to download the following:

Spark: Igniting a Culture of Multiplication by Todd Wilson
Sending Capacity, Not Seating Capacity by J.D. Greear and Mike McDaniel
You Can Multiply Your Church: One Journey to Radical Multiplication by Ralph Moore
Disciplism by Alan Hirsch
Flow: Unleashing a River of Multiplication in Your Church, City and Word by Larry Walkemeyer
The Journey: Toward a Healthy Multiplying Church by Darrin Patrick
Collaboration for Multiplication: The Story of the Houston Church Planting Network by Bruce Wesley
Sending Church: Stories of Momentum and Multiplication by Dan Smith
Together for the City: What Can Happen When the Mission is Bigger than 1 Congregation by Tom Hughes and Kevin Haah
Saturating Austin: A Strategy as Big as Your City by Tim Hawks and John Herrington
Igniting Movements: Multiplying Churches in Dark Places by Dr. Ajai Lall and Josh Howard
Reach: A Story of Multiplication in the City by Brian Bolt
More Than BBQ: How God is Creating a City-Wide Church Planting Movement in Kansas City by Dan Southerland and Troy McMahon
Give God Some Credit: Risk Taking for the Greater Impact by Brett Andrews
Start a Movement, Plant a Church by Josh Burnett
His Burden is Light: Experiencing Multiplication through Letting Go by K.P. Yohannan
Small Church, Big Impact: A Call for Small Churches to Multiply by Kevin Cox

Related Resources

Throughout 2015 and beyond, Exponential will be sharing stories and examples of multiplying churches through this eBook series and via our 2015, 2016 and 2017 Exponential conference themes.

eBooks

20+ new FREE eBooks are being added via this new library. Authors include Larry Walkemeyer, JD Greear, Ralph Moore, KP Yohannan, Ajai Lall, Darrin Patrick, Steve Stroope, and many more. These leaders of multiplying churches will share their journey of creating a culture of multiplication growth.

These eBooks are in addition to 60+ existing FREE eBooks in Exponential's resource library. Check out exponential.org/resource-ebooks to download these books.

Exponential Conferences

The theme of the Exponential 2015 conferences was "SPARK: Igniting a Culture of Multiplication."

The theme of Exponential 2016 is "Becoming a Level Five Multiplying Church." Join thousands of other leaders as we pursue a better understanding of how to leverage our tensions to create and grow a culture of multiplication. Visit exponential.org/events to learn more.

You can also visit exponential.org/digital-access-pass to access content from all 10 main stage sessions from Exponential East 2015 as well as the main stage sessions from Exponential 2016

Social Media

Twitter - @churchplanting
Facebook - Facebook.com/churchplanting
RSS - http://feeds.feedburner.com/exponential

If churches are not prepared for what is here today, how will they respond to what lies ahead? We can still become the Church as it was always meant to be—a rapidly spreading, high impact, movement.

100M begins with Leap Year, a standalone one-year movement accelerator designed to launch your church and its leadership into the basic posture of movement.

◇

Only 100 churches will have a chance to experience this. Are you ready to shift the tracks of church history with us?

◇

Visit 100movements.com
to download more information and get started.

EXPONENTIAL 2017

APRIL 24-27
ORLANDO, FL

DRE∧M
BIG

BE A PART OF THE LARGEST ANNUAL GATHERING
OF CHURCH MULTIPLICATION LEADERS ON THE PLANET!

5000+ Church Multiplication Leaders / 100+ Speakers
100+ Workshops / 10 Tracks
10 Pre-Conference Sessions / Sunny, Florida

EX exponential.org/events

About Todd Wilson

Todd Wilson currently serves as the Director of Exponential (exponential.org) and is founding member of the organization whose core focus is distributing thought leadership through conferences, books, podcasts, software, and small group learning communities.

Todd is passionate about the local church and the starting of healthy, high-impact new churches. He enjoys starting new things focused on Kingdom impact and multiplication, as well as helping others create an image of future possibilities and the strategy to implement them.

Todd received his B.S. in nuclear engineering from North Carolina State University and a master's degree equivalent from the Bettis Atomic Power Laboratory. He spent 15 years serving in the Division of Naval Reactors on nuclear submarine design, operation, maintenance, and overhaul.

After a two-year wrestling match with God, Todd entered full-time vocational ministry as the Executive Pastor at New Life Christian Church where he played a visionary and strategic role for several years as New Life grew and implemented key initiatives such as multisite, externally focused, and church planting. His passion for starting healthy new churches continues to increase, and he now spends most of his energy engaged in a wide range of leading-edge and pioneering initiatives aimed at helping catalyze movements of healthy, reproducing churches.

Todd is a certified Life Planner and strategically invests in the lives of several leaders and organizations each year. He has written/co-written multiple books, including *Stories of Sifted* (with Eric Reiss), *Spark: Igniting a Culture of Multiplication* and *More: Find Your Personal Calling and Live Life to the Fullest Measure*.

Todd lives in Manassas, Virginia, with his wife Anna (happily married for over 25 years) and their two boys, Ben and Chris.

About Dave Ferguson

Dave Ferguson is the lead pastor of Community Christian Church, an innovative multi-site missional community that is passionate about "helping people find their way back to God." Community has grown from a few college friends to thousands every weekend meeting at 13 locations in the Chicago area and has been recognized as one of America's most influential churches.

Dave provides visionary leadership for NewThing, whose mission is to be a catalyst for movements of reproducing churches. He is the president and board chair for Exponential, the largest church planting conference in the world and is on the board of Ministry Grid and Leadership Network.

Dave is also an adjunct professor at Wheaton Graduate School and board member for Leadership Network and for the Institute for Community. He is an award-winning co-author of leadership books, including *The Big Idea* (2007), *Exponential* (2010) *On The Verge* (2011), *Discover Your Mission Now* (2012), *Keeping Score* (2013) and *Finding Your Way Back to God* (2015). Dave has written many articles and spoken worldwide at various leadership and church planting conferences.

Dave received his masters at Wheaton Graduate School; M.A. Educational Ministries—specializing in Church Planting in 1991 and his bachelors from Lincoln Christian University; B.A., Bible and Communications in 1986.

Dave and his wife, Sue, have three children—Amy, Joshua and Caleb—and live in Naperville, Illinois. He loves sports and enjoys reading and running.